MW00445186

My book

of

Potpourri Poetry
Second Edition

Haikus, Kigos, Senryus, Tankas, Katautas, Gogyoshi & Gogyohka, and Sijos

by

Patrick Michael

(placeholder)

Copyright Page

Acknowledgment Page

To all my family and friends who have supported me in my efforts since I started writing poetry in early 2006.

Dedication Page

I stand on the backs of giants who come before me, but in deference to those who have guided and helped me along the way, I dedicate this book of poetry, first of all to my Mother, Dorothy, who passed away in 1994, to my brothers and sister, Bill, Jim and Dixie and to my sons, Sean, Ryan and Scot, my cousin, Mary Adele, my niece, great nieces and nephews, Particularly Michael, also a poet, who also passed suddenly in 2014, as well as close friends who have encouraged me to publish my poetry and provided wonderful inspiration as well, Katherine, Merike, Olga, who helped me tons on my title and offered suggestions, Rachel, Paula, and Swapan, who came up with a name for my own poem style, the Partistanza and many others on poetry sites who I have lost touch with over time.

Table of Contents

1. Lifting Love, pages 1-2
2. Sad Times, pages 3-4
3. Head Over Heels in Love, pages 5-6
4. Bending the Will, pages 7-8
5. Understanding Love, pages 9-10
6. Slings and Arrows, pages 11-12
7. Spreading Love, pages 13-14
8. Self-confidence, pages 15-16
9. Testing the Waters, pages 17-18
10. Tap Dancing, pages 19-20
11. Fast or Slow, pages 21-22
12. Gauges, pages 23-24
13. Tomorrow, pages 25-26
14. Facing Life, pages 27-28
15. Loyalty, pages 29-30
16. Giving Up on Love, pages 31-32
17. Scary Faces, pages 33-34
18. Halloween Voting, pages 35-37
19. Effortless Love, pages 38-39
20. Long Distance Love, pages 40-41
21. Gentile Persuasion, 42-43
22. Moonlight and Love, pages 44-45

Table of Contents

23. Losing Favor, pages 46-47

24. Amazing Grace, pages 48-49

25. The Rapture, pages 50-51

26. Hard Times, pages 52-53

27. Tortured Souls, pages 54-55

28. Crisis of Conscience, pages 56-57

29. Demagogues Need Saints, pages 58-59

30. Passion and Fear, page 60-61

31. Pride and Prejudice, pages 62-63

32. Life Complicates Love, pages 64-65

33. Cyber Play, pages 66-67

34. Lost, pages 68-69

35. Back Pain, pages 70-71

36. Phony Baloney, pages 72-73

37. Murky Waters, Pages 74-75

38. Marking Paths, pages 76-77

39. Scary Places, pages 78-79

40. Loss of Hope, pages 80-81

41. Money, pages 82-83

42. Romantic Waves, pages 84-85

43. Winning a Girl's Heart, pages 86-87

44. Heartstrings, pages 88-89

Table of Contents

45. Cosmic Connections, pages 90-91
46. The Nature of Love, pages 92-93
47. Angelic Souls, pages 94-95
48. Challenging the Soul, pages 96-97
49. Nature's Love, pages 98-99
50. Puberty, pages 100-101
51. Stability, pages 102-103
52. Sensual Passion, pages 104-105
53. Heartbeats, pages 106-107
54. Fame, pages 108-109
55. Agony, pages 110-111
56. Pain and Passion, pages 112-113
57. Generosity of Soul, pages 114-115
58. Dying Passion, pages 116-117
59. Ability to Love, pages 118-119
60. Embracing Love, pages 120-121
61. Magic, pages 122-123
62. Actions, pages 124-125
63. Balanced Souls, pages 126-127
64. Relativity, pages 128-129
65. Hungers, pages 130-131
66. Barriers to Love, pages 132-133

Table of Contents

67. Differences, pages 134-135

68. Fundamental Values, pages 136-137

69. Infatuation, pages 138-140

70. Fluidity, pages 141-143

71. Focusing Love, pages 144-146

72. Myth, pages 147-149

73. Lost Energy, pages 150-152

74. Friends, pages 154-155

75. Forsaken Love, pages 156-158

76. Cosmic Bliss, pages 159-161

78. Conscious Allure, pages 162-164

79. Gender Senses, pages 165-167

80. Dreaming, pages 168-170

81. Long Term Friendship, pages 171-173

82. Cages, pages 174-176

83. Egos, pages 177-179

84. Fun, pages 180-182

85. Reflections, pages 183-185

86. Aging, pages 186-188

87. Duty, pages 189-191

88. My Song, pages 192-194

89. Fear, pages 195-197

90. Fate, pages 198-200

Lifting Love

(A Tanka)

Love is an embrace
of values that do matter
a spirit of true romance
giving and taking with love
lifting love, its pedestal.

Citron-Crested Cockatoo

(A Haiku)

A curious bird
quiet, yet tricky, Citron-
Crested Cockatoo.

Soulful Songs

(A Sonian)

Every soul wants to sing
showing its depths bared
giving sense in
soulful songs.

A Sense of Soul

(A Tideling)

Singing is adventurous
romance shows us sensuous
a sense of soul is fearless.

Romance gives courage

making love to encourage
a sense of soul is fearless.

Dating needs bravery
old times are reverie
a sense of soul is fearless.

The soul wants to be bared
fear keeps us in abeyance.

Love is fearless in hard times
the soul wants a partner in crimes.

Magic of Soul

(A Sijo)

Every soul has its own song, magic embraces deep love
baring the soul is a private and done in romantic settings
the magic soul can be misled, broken hearts need to mend.

Mysticism is part of the feminine soul, enticing love
devil-may-care attitudes may attract women in troves
the magic of soul senses harm, regrets need to be let go.

Seduction is an art pursuing pure satisfaction
nature gives us what we need to entertain deepest love
the magic of soul is uncertain, compassion shows concern.

Sad Times

(A Tanka)

Death is always sad
ill-health harms the spirit
love is primary
compassion embraces us
sad times are part of all lives.

Coral-Billed Pionus

(A Haiku)

A quiet parrot
reserved, a musky odor
Coral-Billed Pionus.

White Fights Black

(A Sonian)

Causes are prolific
too much violence
with bigotry
white fights black.

Bigotry and Hate

(A Tideling)

Resentment is sickening
it leads to bickering
bigotry and hate grow in a dark abyss.

Prejudice is zealotry
it leaves awkward legacy
bigotry and hate grow in a dark abyss.

Discrimination is harmful
zealotry becomes too scornful
bigotry and hate grow in a dark abyss.

Chauvinism breeds greed and hate
resentment creates anger and racism.

White communities are hypocritic
avoiding being empathetic.

Creating Sources of Love

(A Sijo)

We all grow upon fake impressions based on our parenting
peer pressure takes a toll on how we feel about others
creating sources of love is hard, let go of false impressions.

Closed minds breed hate n' anger, compassion is needed
group thinking is almost always off base, think for yourself
using words of love can be hurt, show charm n' give love.

Prejudice is bred mostly in homes where the legacy is hate
bigotry is ignorant and fails the test of enlightenment
creating sources of love gets shunned, let go of your anger.

Head Over Heels in Love

(A Tanka)

Romance can seduce
the mind and heart to give in
to words and actions
embraced by depths of the soul
when head over heels in love.

Crimson Rosella

(A Haiku)

A bird needing love
pretty, territorial
Crimson Rosella.

Age and Love

(A Sonian)

Age is just a number
maturity counts
women ignore
age with love.

Evil Ways

(A Tideling)

Malevolence is diabolical
the devil is methodical
evil ways thrive on the dark side.

Demonic beliefs plague
the soul becomes vague
evil ways thrive on the dark side.

Immorality becomes vicious
making actions more pernicious
evil ways thrive on the dark side.

The dark side needs light to shine
evil hides in the shadows of time.

Love will overcome evil
if compassion becomes civil.

Malevolence

(A Sijo)

Wickedness comes in many forms, good can overcome
demons hide in the shadows of time, darkness evades
malevolence seeks to do harm, resentment to alarm.

Passion can lead to anger, to hate others over time
struggles make us impatient, our passion may explode
malevolence grows in the mind, demons will do us harm.

Broken hearts can lead to hate, compassion will be needed
to avoid the dark side during the twilight of overcoming
malevolence is a broken spirit, the death of what is prime.

Bending the Will

(A Tanka)

Seduction seeks love
romancing by building trust
showing real patience
taking the time to entice
bending the will to love's task.

Collared Aracari

(A Haiku)

A friendly, calm bird
tricks well and loves to cuddle
Collared Aracari.

Letting Children Grow

(A Sonian)

It is easy to squeeze
making kids feel soft
parents should let
children grow.

Growth and Love

(A Tideling)

Letting children mature
part of parenting nature
growth and love mean letting go.

Nurturing dependents graciously
helping them overcome naivety
growth and love mean letting go.

Adulthood is maturity
age leads to annuity
growth and love mean letting go.

Age is just a number
maturity is more worthwhile.

Growing up means enlightened living
letting go leads to children thriving.

Confidence in Love

(A Sijo)

Young ones need confidence to gain maturity in life
letting nature teaches them helps them know good living
confidence in love can get us hurt, yet letting go helps us.

Children need enlightenment and encouragement to thrive
shaming only works when their acts stop the harm
confidence in love can break a heart, charm is a blessing.

Nurturing Children is a tough job, all parents need to learn
teaching skills come with the trials of giving love, empathy
trust in love has pitfalls, teach your kids, giving them love.

Understanding Love

(A Tanka)

The cosmos connects
everything and everyone
regrets interfere
with this cosmic love blessing
understanding love goes slow.

Crimson-Bellied Conure

(A Haiku)

Playful, quiet bird
with a good temper, Crimson-
Bellied Conures thrive.

Confusion

(A Sonian)

Changes come frequently
without a notice
causing the mind
confusion.

Traveling

(A Tideling)

Airline travel deludes
give people poor attitudes
traveling is an adventure.

Sailing is adventurous

jibing requires more dexterous
traveling is an adventure.

Driving is hazardous
the scenery is glamorous
traveling is an adventure.

Each journey has a life of its own
changes happen in free form.

Adventures should be carefree
traveling should give us esprit.

Fixing Irregularities

(A Sijo)

To fix problems, you first try to understand what caused it
as you must interpret the fix correctly to know the solution
fixing irregularities can cause more problems, be patient.

Solutions can be difficult to find with sites poorly designed
praying may keep your peace of mind, if you fix problems
fixing irregularities can do you harm, mind how you solve it.

Men may think they can fix all problems, a laugh is refined
girls like to think they can fix men, who pay them no mind
fixing faults can break the heart, protect yourself first.

Slings and Arrows

(A Tanka)

Misfortune is hell
but it doesn't have to be
regrets may haunt us
letting go helps rid us of
slings and arrows that do harm.

Curl-Crested Aracari

(A Haiku)

Long beaked, friendly bird
quiet, good with tricks, a Curl-
Crested Aracari.

Waterfalls

(A Sonian)

Rain is a source of change
the sound of raindrops
bodes of crashing
waterfalls.

Waterwings

(A Tideling)

Soaring requires airfoils
floating on cloudy gargoyles
waterwings make us buoyant.

Lifting capacity embraces

depth of physical graces
waterwings make us buoyant.

Diving requires awareness
a sensing of sereneness
waterwings make us buoyant.

Water is a source of cleansing
the body and soul need it.

Refreshing the soul requires more
meditation may even the score.

Cleansing the Soul

(A Sijo)

Wind, fire and water help fulfill many of all mankind's needs
meditating helps bring us peace of mind, let go of regrets
cleansing the soul is not harmful, renewal is always helpful.

Winds adjust with no notice, it can be good or evil
fire keeps us warm n' allows us to cook our food to nourish
cleansing a soul for a broken heart is a drug for ills of mind.

Water is for cleansing bodies, both inside, out, cook as well
peace of mind comes if we feel happy on how we are living
cleansing a soul is a struggle to learn, on happy choices.

Spreading Love

(A Tanka)

Replenishing love
takes patience, understanding
to increase romance
building trust of each other
spreading love through children born.

Ducorp's Cockatoo

(A Haiku)

Intelligent bird
good talking ability
Ducorp's Cockatoo.

Encouraging Love's Embrace

(A Sonian)

Romance is beginning
a trust in someone
encouraging
love's embrace.

Developing True Love

(A Tideling)

Romance is subscribing
to trust and guiding
developing true love as time passes.

Providing for another

ensuring not to smother
developing true love as time passes.

Building a relationship
requires a long courtship
developing true love as time passes.

True love is not easy
building trust takes time.

Developing love is romantic
focus is on not being frantic.

Time Well Spent

(A Sijo)

Though time is a variable, it can easily be wasted
children need attention till they learn to manage their time
time well spent can be hazardous, there are always pitfalls.

Wasting time of others is not useful, and is not well spent
the boss should know to spend time better than workers
time well spent can leave regrets, love shown has respect.

Family needs come first, friends and others fit in thereafter
lovers need attention, making love is new beginning
time well spent is harder, practice does not make perfect.

Self-Confidence

(A Tanka)

Lack of confidence
will kill the spirit of love
depression sets in
building a vicious circle
self-confidence spreads romance.

Masked Lovebird

(A Haiku)

A quiet, nest bird
tricky, territorial
is a masked lovebird.

Confidence

(A Sonian)

Self-esteem builds strong souls
shame kills the spirit
we all need self
confidence.

Building Self-Confidence

(A Tideling)

Self-esteem needs promotion
shame creates inner commotion
building self-confidence needs enchantment.

Expectations breed uncertainty

following trends is absurdity
building self-confidence needs enchantment.

Personalities are different
passions create our interest
building self-confidence needs enchantment.

Differences are what counts
similarities are boring.

Love helps build competence
as we are building self-confidence.

Shame
(A Sijo)

Kids need to feel good of themselves, to give them courage
self-esteem grows with rewards for meeting expectations
shame breaks the inner spirit, with loss of self-confidence.

Growth needs urging, to build passions for enlightenment
love must be part of the life, proving knowledge to know
shame is a tool of last resort, be careful how you use it.

Each journey has a life of its own, we may watch its fruition
nature is there to teach us, lessons we learn help us grow
shame will do harm, be sure you know the end game.

Testing the Waters

(A Tanka)

Dating can be hot
especially with one you like
placing trust in them
baring souls romantically
testing the waters of love.

Dusky Lory

(A Haiku)

A high pitched squealer
talks well and shows its beauty
a Dusky Lory.

Sharing Love

(A Sonian)

Families are capable
of giving, taking
promotion of
sharing love.

Grace and Love

(A Tideling)

Romance becomes graceful
when trust is faithful
grace and love need patience.

Dating affords practice

in not being tactless
grace and love need patience.

Refinement takes elegance
in giving it relevance
grace and love need patience.

Tact shows you have common sense
manners are part of being graceful.

Love needs grace and trust to last
for real reverie to be cast.

Acceptance

(A Sijo)

Self aware takes time to gain wisdom and enlightenment
anxiety creates a struggle within, overcome with patience
acceptance by others is problematic, develop your soul.

When young we want to fit in, and do well in life and love
learning of nature helps us grow and mature more rapidly
acceptance helps to overcome the strain, letting go regrets.

Age does not always bring wisdom, lessons of nature flow
to give peace of mind, some things we are never will know
acceptance is not always good, evil is the undertow.

Tap Dancing

(A Tanka)

Fakes like advantage
taking, not having to give
wanting sex players
no love or relationships
tap dancing their way through life.

Dusky Pionus

(A Haiku)

A low noise parrot
aggressive and quite playful
Dusky Pionus.

Life with Love

(A Sonian)

Life requires stamina
love requires real trust
for a chance at
life with love.

Sleeping It Off

(A Tideling)

Everyone needs recuperation
after a day's degradation
sleeping it off makes you feel human.

Cultivating life's ambitions
requires effort in competitions
sleeping it off makes you feel human.

Aspirations need creativity
strenuous work needs sensitivity
sleeping it off makes you feel human.

Hard work requires plenty of rest
a hard day's night comes quickly.

Rest and recuperation take time
a good sleep keeps us in our prime.

Enjoying Life

(A Sijo)

Stress is a killer, it destroys happiness in too many lives
patience takes time to bring peace through apt meditation
enjoy life, don't struggle, let go regrets, gain peace of mind.

Nerves develop over time, learn to mediate to bring peace
work balancing play keeps us feeling the best, in our prime
enjoying life has pitfalls, overcome hurdles to protect souls.

Broken hearts can be overcome, love is fragile in our youth
nature teaches us lessons as we grow, if we pay attention
enjoying life can bring harm, so pay attention to your soul.

Fast or Slow

(A Tanka)

Rushing is funky
nothing will be gained with speed
love is enchanting
when couples test their limits
fast or slow, find leisurely.

Dusky-Head Conure

(A Haiku)

Playful, active bird
that screeches for attention
Dusky-Head Conure.

Meditation Shapes the Soul

(A Sonian)

Souls have predilections
winds of change must blow
meditation
shapes the soul.

Transcending the Dark

(A Tideling)

Darkness is provocative
as enlightenment is cognitive
transcending the dark finds true love.

Nebulous is evocative
of what is causative
transcending the dark finds true love.

Romance is demonstrative
making love is expressive
transcending the dark finds true love.

The twilight brings moonbeams
love is romantic enchantment.

In the dark we find the limelight
transcending the dark with moonlight.

Transcending the Dark

(A Sijo)

In the shadows of our lives thrives a darkness to overcome
when we are filled with regrets, we must mediate and let go
transcending dark can do harm, we must strive to find love.

When young we hold bad dreams, aging can give wisdom
in the dark we grow beyond our wildest imaginations
transcending dark outwits us, to overcome fears gives love.

Basking in the sunshine gives us a feeling of enlightenment
yet we need truth and trust to grow a real, abiding wisdom
transcending the dark is sowing of wild oats, yielding love.

Gauges

(A Tanka)

We all use measures
to see how we feel of friends
romanticizing
with one we want to be with
our gauges sometimes fail us.

Duyvenbody's Lory

(A Haiku)

Entertaining Bird
that is loud, Duyvenbody's
Lory is hand tamed.

Devotion to All of Life

(A Sonian)

Life is self-dependent
we all need strong love
devotion to
all of life.

Gauging Self-Worth

(A Tideling)

Degrees of independence
depend on feeling confidence
gauging self-worth requires a sound soul.

Anxieties become problematic

making us more fanatic
gauging self-worth requires a sound soul.

Loving Mothers' devotion
is a love potion
gauging self-worth requires a sound soul.

We all need sex to survive
we thrive on deep inner love.

We criticize ourselves in growing up
gauging self-worth is a checkup.

Fomenting Lies
(A Sijo)

Some folks build on their own lies, like it will never matter
they believe in conspiracy theories and treat others badly
building lies does harm, as sound minds overcome them.

We all tell little white lies in building relationships
when we bare our souls, the truth is cherished for all time
pushing lies destroys relationships, do not waste our time.

The politics of love is devotion to each other
when we are devoted, nothing can break a lover's charm
fomenting lies is evil, enchantment is a deep love.

Tomorrow

(A Tanka)

We have the moment
in it we can work or play
we should enjoy it
no matter what comes of it
tomorrow is not aware.

Emerald Toucanet

(A Haiku)

Intelligent bird
mountainous, quiet, tricky
Emerald Toucanet.

Giving and Taking

(A Sonian)

Romance is sporadic
patience brings a laugh
love is giving
and taking.

Moonlight and Chi

(A Tideling)

Moonlight is enchanting
the soul seeks everlasting
moonlight and chi embrace love.

Romance is passionate
the heart seeks compassionate
moonlight and chi embrace love.

Twilight is romantic
making love is frantic
moonlight and chi embrace love.

Moonbeams and starlight shining
make romance seem charismatic.

Love needs enthusiasm
chi gives energy like plasm.

Open Love

(A Sijo)

Love needs passion and openness to let go of regrets
pain and struggles are part of any real relationship
open love has pitfalls, spending time together equals two.

The eyes are the path to the soul, love makes them sparkle
dating helps build trust and a sound relationship to grow on
open love can lead to broken hearts, wisdom builds trust.

Moonlight is loving, making love brings sparkles to the eyes
passion is giving from the heart and soul, being romantic
open love may cause fights, we should know to love well.

Facing Life

(A Tanka)

Life is a struggle
standing on your own two feet
is hard for some folks
money makes it easier
facing life gives self-esteem.

English Type Budgie

(A Haiku)

A bird kept for show
a chatterbox and playful
English Type Budgie.

Rainy Days

(A Sonian)

Cloudy skies bring us rain
sometimes drenching us
dancing comes with
rainy days.

Mystical Forces

(A Tideling)

Romance is whimsical
gratification can be inexplicable
mystical forces must connect with the cosmos.

Dating builds relationships
making love is companionship
mystical forces must connect with the cosmos.

Passion is enchantment
love develops an attachment
mystical forces must connect with the cosmos.

The cosmos connects us all
both animals and people.

Forces of love are mystical
merging of souls is empirical.

Cloudy Days
(A Sijo)

Clouds come for all areas of the world, no matter the lands
some places are very arid, others rain comes everyday
cloudy days harm plans, make plans ahead of time wisely.

Black clouds bring rain, thunder claps are reason for pain
storms can drench grounds, some can cause lands to flood
cloudy days can bring harm to lands, if it rains awfully hard.

Rain clouds get dark as they fill with dew, dancing on roofs
puddles are for splashing in, no matter what the time of day
cloudbursts seem to hurt the ears, rain is to play the day.

Loyalty

(A Tanka)

Life is a struggle
families, blood relations first
love is a bastion
of freedom for a good soul
loyalty comes when deserved.

Fife Canary

(A Haiku)

Active, singing bird
timid and good for a pet
the Fife Canary.

Shackles of Love

(A Sonian)

Romance is not easy
love needs to build trust
shackles of love
we resist.

Barriers to Romance

(A Tideling)

Dating is problematic
making up is traumatic
barriers to romance can be overcome.

Passion is ecstatic

hugs and kisses, emphatic
barriers to romance can be overcome.

Embraces are melodramatic
changes can be erratic
barriers to romance can be overcome.

Life is a struggle
we juggle our schedules.

Still barriers make us turn away
romance does not mean we will stay.

The Thrust of Romance

(A Sijo)

Dating is meant to build a relationship with love and trust
passion builds over time if the cosmos brings forces in tune
the thrust of love can be spoiled, if cheating is rampant.

Passion is required if the relationship is meant to last
trust must be emphasized, as romance is an adventure
the thrust of romance can do damage, so watch every step.

A fling is not meant to be permanent, love is a commitment
love needs embraces, hugs and kisses to keep love flowing
the thrust of love has killed, let go regrets to have it last.

Giving Up on Love

(A Tanka)

Women feel love's pain
get broken hearts easily
trying to care more
finding a good man to love
giving up on love in time.

Senegal Parrot

(A Haiku)

A colorful bird
they can learn to mimic talk
Senegal Parrot.

Machinations

(A Sonian)

Intrigue is all romance
adventures take strength
machinations
bring passion.

Passion

(A Tideling)

Romance becomes intriguing
desires can be fatiguing
passion will keep us focused.

Dating inspires adventure
making love is splendor
passion will keep us focused.

Seduction is romantic
lessons learned are pedantic
passion will keep us focused.

Inner depths hold our souls
passion comes from there.

Cosmic bliss is deep passion
enticing us to show compassion.

Obituaries

(A Sijo)

We all live so that we may make the wisest achievements
living and learning from nature as we gain inner wisdom
obituaries posted for our death, make a worthy tombstone.

Crime and punishment make a bad fit, creating scandal
love is given by most Mothers, setting a good example
obituaries express good and bad, we all need compassion.

Romance may lead to a sound relationship, do your best
to stand on your own two feet, forget about all regrets
obituaries can show the dark side, find your own light.

Scary Faces

(A Tanka)

The face of love thrives
when fear and regrets grow numb
we struggle with love
broken hearts are quite common
scary faces are love's pain.

Blue-Fronted Amazon

(A Haiku)

A talking parrot
they bond with one person, Blue-
Fronted Amazon.

The Haunting

(A Sonian)

Halloween brings twilight
moonlight brings werewolves
ghouls and goblins
the haunting.

Ghosts and Goblins

(A Tideling)

Halloween is suspenseful
witches can be vengeful
ghosts and goblins come but once a year.

Werewolves are bloodthirsty

the darkness is worthy
ghosts and goblins come but once a year.

Forests are exciting
sprites and faeries inviting
ghosts and goblins come but once a year.

Halloween only comes once a year
demons may gobble you up in between.

Ghosts and goblins hide in gaps of the mind
suspense brings them out when you feel maligned.

Haunting the Soul

(A Sijo)

Halloween is full of heart n' soul n' decadent enchantment
ghosts, goblins, sprites n' faeries to fill kids on sheer delight
haunting souls of them bitten by werewolves, n' banshees.

Halloween starts the day intense, the soul awaits the night
eagerness fills the mind and heart, candy is the enticement
haunting the soul of kiddies, they yearn for wild excitement.

The darkness hides with inner depths of the soul, as a bite
vampires with whites of their eyes bloodthirsty at twilight
haunting souls of damsels in distress, for love of moonlight.

Halloween Voting

(A Senryu)

Trump is a twerkey
the G O P is spooky
please vote your conscience.

Spooky Love

(A Tanka)

Goblins will inspire
holding the girl in your arms
the moonlight shines down
as werewolves howl in twilight
spooky love is most profound.

Spooks and Romance

(A Sonian)

Goblins and ghosts are spooks
hold your girlfriend tight
make love, Happy
Halloween.

Beetle Halloween

(A Haiku)

Beetles are gremlins
denizens from on the ground
Happy Halloween.

Twilight and Love

(A Tanka)

Werewolves love the night
preying on young necks for blood
drinking like their gin
loving moonlight and bright stars
twilight and love keep them strong.

Roots

(A Haiku)

Herbs are mystical
good health is primal instinct
roots of Halloween.

Devil Roots

(A Sonian)

Ghosts come from ancient forms
on Halloween they
take human form
devil roots.

Ghost Forces

(A Tideling)

Ancients are gigantic
their echos are romantic
ghost forces become arcane.

Ages are eulogized

dictators doing harm despised
ghost forces become arcane.

Halloween is spooky
kids run around kooky
ghost forces become arcane.

Death comes to one and all
life forces we should beware.

No one chooses to be a ghost
Halloween is a twilight host.

Haunted Castles

(A Sijo)

Castles of old are haunted by ancients who like to be scary
as cold barren walls of stone, castles make kids scream
haunted castles draw banshees near, for haunting howling.

High towers keep damsel's fits, Rapunzel is an ancient one
the forces of devilish demons hide in the shadows within
haunted castles are dangerous, be careful where you walk.

The ramparts of bridges to castles over moats are scary
Hounds of Baskerville troll the edges of dark, teeth bared
haunted castles are scary, demons call Happy Halloween.

Effortless Love

(A Tanka)

Inhale and exhale
breathing easy brings a pause
a moment well spent
brings passion to resonate
effortless love, soft to appease.

Fancy Parakeet

(A Haiku)

A bird loves to charm
a natural clown which climbs, a
fancy parakeet.

Moody Waters

(A Sonian)

Elections bring weird gloom
a sense of losing
moody times cause
eyes to tears.

Tears and Fears

(A Tideling)

Paranoia causes anxiety
romance may hide gravity
tears and fears bring out rivalry.

Tension is foreboding
struggling we are unloading
tears and fears bring out rivalry.

Appetite is uncertain
bargaining is a burden
tears and fears bring out rivalry.

Fears come from depths of the soul
we cry when we sense depression.

Tears come when we feel deep pain
the heart is about to break, insane,

Fraud and Love

(A Sijo)

Fraud covers a wide swath across the spectrum our lives
love of family is precious, giving us strength, how we thrive
fraud n' love can do harm, face your soul as you grow old.

Wealth is a valuable asset, charity shows compassion
envy is a conscious desire to own what others have
fraud and love struggle with each other, the heart is fragile.

Greed is a politicians path to get into your wallet
protect what you have and be generous with what you give
fraud n' love can break you, show love as others deserve it.

Long Distance Love

(A Tanka)

Time and patience draw
on one's inner strength to share
feelings of romance
space is an obstacle when
long distance love is involved.

Bluffon's Macaw Bird

(A Haiku)

A docile mixture
of blue and gold, well speaking
Bluffon's Macaw Bird.

Treasured Love

(A Sonian)

Love is not a distance
it travels across
the cosmic sphere
treasured love.

Sinking Dimensions

(A Tideling)

Time becomes meaningless
when we lose faithfulness
sinking dimensions embrace our souls.

Space becomes transcendental

when we hold sentimental
sinking dimensions embrace our souls.

Cosmic friction develops
when we become jealous
sinking dimensions embrace our souls.

Time is a relative dimension
we seek to find our universal place.

Inner demons will make us sink
into nether worlds, making us blink.

Losing Sense of Self

(A Sijo)

Self-esteem is hard to hold onto, so stay self aware
work and play hard as long as possible, to know yourself
losing sense of self happens often, balance is the solution.

Life is a struggle quite often, find balance in cosmic bliss
study nature to learn valuable lessons, and learn them well
losing sense of self may hurt you, mediate, stay self aware.

Love is what we try to hold onto, butterflies are always free
give love to get it back, bare the soul if you get your mate
losing sense of self hurts, get help if you feel depression.

Gentile Persuasion

(A Tanka)

Romance seduces
mind, body and soul to sense
the dark side of love
passion grows to be sublime
gentile persuasion embraced.

Calico Macaw

(A Haiku)

Two species are bred
to gain this beautiful bird
Calico Macaw.

Gentleness

(A Sonian)

Passion can be cruel
love making, wicked
building trust needs
gentleness.

Silent Goals

(A Tideling)

Sounds generate vibrations
the universe gives expectations
silent goals come from the cosmos.

Romance begins relations
in time come frustrations
silent goals come from the cosmos.

Seduction brings admiration
love making brings aspiration
silent goals come from the cosmos.

Goals thrive in the subconscious
silently expressed over time.

Silence will speak mystically
true love is given altruistically.

Silent Persuasion

(A Sijo)

Hand in hand we stroll into the darkness of ambition
we seek love, we strive to seduce one we find attractive
silent faith is a trial by fires of deep passion.

Romance is an opportunity to meet those of our passion
the gentle soul is looking for love in all the wrong places
silent faith can take us down a wrong path, watch for signs.

In work and play we meet folks, we checkout each other
hoping to be blessed by the cosmos, finding love quickly
silent faith hides on the dark side, watch with confidence.

Moonlight and Love

(A Tanka)

Love is light embraced
the moon is partnered with night
we give and we take
in romantic overtones
moonlight and love are blessings.

Catalina Macaw

(A Haiku)

A large, talking bird
a social Catalina
Macaw with beauty.

Buoyant Love

(A Sonian)

Music enhances love
romance embraces
the best part of
buoyant love.

Buoyancy of Romance

(A Tideling)

Rainbows are introspective
watching gives a perspective
buoyancy of romance is cosmic.

Laughter is progressive
love grows when reflective
buoyancy of romance is cosmic.

Pleasure is retrospective
making love is objective
buoyancy of romance is cosmic.

Making love flow requires passion
buoyancy is good for building trust.

Romance is building a relationship
buoyancy brings brinkmanship.

Building a Love Relationship

(A Sijo)

Romance begins a love relationship, gentle makes it real
building trust is complementary give and take for a couple
building a love relationship can fail, failing is part of life.

Trust is a must, all relationships fail due to failures in trust
building strong relationships is passion with heart and soul
building a romance can do harm, watch how you proceed.

Buoyancy is important to a strong relationship
laughter, emotions keep love alive when times are tough
building a romance can hurt feelings, show some charm.

Losing Favor

(A Tanka)

Rigid ideas
cause loss of genuineness
romance tends to die
when little remains to love
losing favor is love's loss.

Indian Ringneck Parakeet

(A Haiku)

Excellent talker
happy as an Indian
Ringneck Parakeet.

Dark Souls

(A Sonian)

Each soul has a blessing
some see light in all
the twilight thrives
in dark souls.

Sexual Prowess

(A Tideling)

Romance needs lovemaking
the moonlight is pulsating
sexual prowess is a blessing.

Roles are complementary
helping should be supplementary
sexual prowess is a blessing.

Children learn elementary
growing into their itinerary
sexual prowess is a blessing.

Sexual play is a healthy goal
without it nothing is as good.

Ecstasy is rapture of the soul
sexual prowess gives us control.

Sex and Love

(A Sijo)

Love without sex abandons the soul, letting go of the mind
the mind is the real sex machine, it helps us do the grind
sex and love can do harm, as without it we would fade.

Religion can kill sexual prowess, letting go of love
we all need sex to be healthy, celibacy is not good for love
sex and love bring kids, with parents love and cherishing.

Sexual prowess keeps us strong, intellect is proof of love
nature is a blessing, teaching us about love and our role
sex and love may push us, be patient to make love last.

Amazing Grace

(A Tanka)

Love is Mother's goal
to teach babies how to live
the give and take of living
developing talents for
amazing grace to embrace.

Fischer's Lovebird

(A Haiku)

A gentle manner
a bird having a shrill chirp
Fischer's Lovebird.

Holding Love in the Heart

(A Sonian)

Romance is a blessing
embracing fondness
within the heart
holding love.

Souls in Grace

(A Tideling)

Mortals become shadows
of souls we juxtapose
souls in grace are compassionate.

Psyches assume roleplaying

usurping what is portraying
souls in grace are compassionate.

Living becomes socialization
devotion is a foundation
souls in grace are compassionate.

Love is a Mother's blessing
children grow accordingly.

Families need a sense of grace
we all need a sense of our space.

The Nature of the Soul
(A Sijo)

The soul hides in the shadows of our subconscious being
Mother's love gives us a place to grow to maturity
the nature of the soul can do us harm, when it is bared.

Each soul is special, its path is held deep within our being
our social being is restrained to hide who we really are
the nature of the soul is wicked, barbaric when we let go.

The soul needs passion, and love to be bared in its role
children need love and nurturing to grow healthy and wise
the nature of the soul is ruthless at times, it will not show.

The Rapture

(A Tanka)

Love lies in the depths
first love is like an earthquake
rattling emotions
shaking the soul's foundation
the rapture compels the soul.

Peregrine Falcon

(A Haiku)

Predatory birds
that require careful handling
Peregrine Falcon.

Ravishing the Soul

(A Sonian)

The soul has a deep depth
love raises desires
the soul requires
ravishing.

A Beautiful Soul

(A Tideling)

Spirits are mystifying
love making is gratifying
a beautiful soul is a blessing.

Passions are creative

peace is meditative
a beautiful soul is a blessing.

Essences stretch reality
romance is a repartee
a beautiful soul is a blessing.

The soul stretches to great depth
the mind tries to maintain control.

Beauty is in the eye if the beholder
love should grow as we get older.

Breaking the Rules

(A Sijo)

Rules are made to regulate behavior in society
the soul fights against a tight of control if we want to live
breaking rules can get us hurt, be careful of your choices.

Businesses need control, otherwise they take advantage
patience is a factor in all that we do, do not lose control
breaking rules causes some harm, so be careful if you do.

Synergy is based on rules of culture as we grow older
the depths of the soul control how we fit in as we mature
breaking the rules is lighting a fire, have an extinguisher.

Hard Times

(A Tanka)

Age is a number
times are hard for the poorest
people who share some
can have no regrets in life
of what they have, not selfish.

Cosmic Blessings

(A Sonian)

Life has a way to change
results of the tides
of good blessings
cosmically.

Love and Money

(A Tideling)

Investments are relative
to interest so tentative
love and money are partners in crime.

Assets build relationships
growing with the companionship
love and money are partners in crime.

Commitment is devotion
romance, a love potion
love and money are partners in crime.

Money gets in the way of romance
love needs a sense of devotion.

Devotion needs a sense of love
the cosmos connects thereof.

The Limits of Love

(A Sijo)

Love is a cosmic connection with romance in the bargain
stretching limits of the mind and heart, with the soul in tow
the limits of love can break, devotion can make you crow.

The cosmos tries to keep us all connected, love is mystical
making love is ecstasy in action, strengthening devotion
the limits of love can be harmed, do not let money defeat it.

Dating is romantic, it takes money to be most charming
patience is a blessing, building trust is the best path to take
the limits of love can go quickly, let go when this happens.

Tortured Souls

(A Tanka)

A soul needs real love
when love is lost on your path
the heart is broken
depression can fill the mind
tortured souls are left to fend.

Australian King Parrot

(A Haiku)

A large, gentle bird
with good mime speech, Australian
King Parrots will bond.

Healthy Love

(A Sonian)

Health becomes essential
with romance in hand
disease may harm
healthy love.

Maintaining Strength

(A Tideling)

Disease becomes problematic
when life is climactic
maintaining strength requires proper nurturing.

Ill-health is misery

based on medical history
maintaining strength requires proper nurturing.

Diagnosis realizes paradigm
torturing the soul's prime
maintaining strength requires proper nurturing.

Strength is a blessing in life
disease robs us of real strength.

Medicine is a science and practice
nurturing love needs good tactics.

Patience and Health

(A Sijo)

Health and romance make life easier for most of society
disease brings a need for strength and patience with reality
patience and health may go, be healthy if you have choice.

Immunological diseases are hard to lose, there is loss
of strength and utility, being healthy is a blessing
patience and health can be lost, brush teeth for good care.

Diet is good for health and strength, watch what you eat
have good habits on life's path, know what you are doing
patience and health can be lost, meditate in some ways.

Crisis of Conscience

(A Tanka)

Minds are often strange
leaning to biased old frames
anger and hate burn
the compassion for money
crisis of conscience is pain.

Bourke's Parakeet

(A Haiku)

A smart, friendly bird
non-talking, bathing daily
the Bourke's Parakeet.

A Crisis of the Conscience

(A Sonian)

Politics, religions
bring frustrations out
a crisis of
the conscience.

Politics, Religion and Money

(A Tideling)

Crisis brings frustration
love loses its foundation
politics, religion and money can cause harm.

Temptation is fundamental

to nature so elemental
politics, religion and money can cause harm.

Behaviors bring criticism
anger and hate egoism
politics, religion and money can cause harm.

Bigotry is always harmful
religion and politics do harm.

Love is a cosmic blessing
money is never caressing.

Proof in the Pudding
(A Sijo)

Life is a real struggle to find truth in a field of lies
we will reach a crisis of conscience when we feel let down
proof of pudding can sow pain, do care what you hope for.

Politics, religion fight for power, money partners with fame
love gets lost in the equation, a crisis in the cosmos
proof in the pudding tastes sour, if life goes in the drain.

Greed in politics makes strange bed fellows, hate is painful
the stress we deal with in hard times is a problem, meditate
proof in the pudding can bring doubts, clarify your needs.

Demagogues Need Saints

(A Tanka)

Trash talk is okay
for demagogues to make speech
belittling the weak
taking money for the rich
demagogues need saints to sate.

Blossom Headed Parakeet

(A Haiku)

A shy, quiet bird
with good miming skills, Blossom
Headed Parakeet.

Demagogues

(A Sonian)

Money makes demons become
hungry for known saints
to satisfy
demagogues.

Saints

(A Tideling)

Politics is divisive
making people seem derisive
saints work hard to keep the peace.

Demagogues are demons

hungry for all reasons
saints work hard to keep the peace.

Religion, a battleground
for righteous folks, profound
saints work hard to keep the peace.

Politics and religion do not mix
anger always comes into play.

Love is a blessing
saints are caressing.

Saints Defy Demagogues

(A Sijo)

Demagogues hunger for money, like demons in the night
ill-health can pull demagogues down, cheats cannot give in
saints defy demagogues, may be harmed, do stay by them.

Demagogues will lie and cheat to gain their satisfaction
making pain for others, misery they want in their shame
saints defy demagogues, get hurt, yet give back anyway.

Demagogues are liars, bigots, no good flows in their veins
hate feeds their souls, money makes their pain go away
saints defy demagogues, aching for folks, help good work.

Passion and Fear

(A Tanka)

Death comes to us all
love, fears we must overcome
are part of struggles
we fight within our closed minds
passion and fear, wild winds blow.

Barraband Parakeet

(A Haiku)

A colony bird
noisy are the Barraband
Parakeet is cute.

Circles

(A Sonian)

Life is but a circle
with living comes death
vicious paths bring
dark circles.

Romantic Circles

(A Tideling)

Romance needs adulation
giving and taking inflation
romantic circles are magical.

Dating has consequences
love making causes expenses
romantic circles are magical.

Relationships are expensive
love is always intensive
romantic circles are magical.

Life is but a circle
death comes at the end.

Life can be a vicious circle
hold onto love within, vernal.

Trusting the Soul
(A Sijo)

The soul is our guide throughout lives, giving us real hope
we go to school to learn rules to be followed for some time
trusting the soul can lead to harm, nature can enthrall.

The subconscious is also a guide if sleeping brings real
when we learn from our dreams, we live in the soul's light
trusting souls can get us hurt, lessons come with that price.

Depths of the soul are gender biased, genes change roles
romance leads us astray, heart and soul lead us to heaven
trusting the soul is hazardous, not trusting is an evil curse.

Pride and Prejudice

(A Tanka)

Proud is sometimes good
but stereotyping stinks
love is compassion
frustration causes mistakes
pride and prejudice destroy.

American Singer Canary

(A Haiku)

A bird with sweet chirps
singing tweets, American
Singer Canary.

Laughter Nurtures the Soul

(A Sonian)

Happiness is a choice
jokes help nurture
laughter nurtures
every soul.

Precious Moments

(A Tideling)

Reverie is prophetic
romance is sometimes poetic
precious moments help keep us lively.

Weddings are synesthetic

energizing hearts to aesthetic
precious moments help keep us lively.

Making love copacetic
taking hearts to parthenogenetic
precious moments help keep us lively.

Romance gives us experience
in relationship building.

Love needs compassion to grow
precious moments are seeds to sow.

Failing the Relationship

(A Sijo)

Anger and resentment give license to failures all the time
one sided ambitions make life difficult, for the family
failing the relationship hurts everyone, think before you act.

Selfishness is harmful, childish and leaves us few choices
placing yourself before folks is weak that tries to control
failing the relationship always harms, a time to let go.

Pride and prejudice do not mix well, and love cannot flow
romance is part of loving, ventures help our souls to glow
failing the relationship is hurtful, calmness helps the soul.

Life Complicates Love

(A Tanka)

Life is a struggle
multifaceted in ways
it keeps us busy
our souls need a break sometimes
life complicates love and life.

Canary Winged Parakeet

(A Haiku)

An agile, nervous
bird that can talk, Canary
Winged Parakeet chirps.

Wheat from Chaff

(A Sonian)

Life is a blossoming
we struggle living
separating
wheat from chaff.

Life and Willpower

(A Tideling)

Perseverance is commitment
for which thrives fulfillment
life and willpower, the soul's foundation.

Courage gives tenacity
living gives us vivacity
life and willpower, the soul's foundation.

Resourcefulness breeds creativity
developing our true proclivity
life and willpower, the soul's foundation.

Life is a creative process
nature teaches us many lessons.

Love gives us true compassion
willpower shows our attraction.

Give and Take

(A Sijo)

All relationships require a solid foundation to last
each party must show willpower for true perseverance
give and take avoids love being broken, show compassion.

Creativity gives each a foundation of love, so do your best
work and play hard, and give weight to your words if wrong
give and take make paths that may be painful, if you err.

Romance is a time for charm and passion, do your best
to keep love alive in the relationship, keep willpower strong
give and take build issues, avoid making them problems.

Cyber Play

(A Tanka)

Bullying is real
politics comes into play
compassion is love
hate and anger will destroy
cyber play can be cruel.

Brown-Throated Conure

(A Haiku)

An affectionate
well talking, a Brown-Throated
Conure pet.

Compatibility

(A Sonian)

Matches made in heaven
compatibility
grows due to love's
persuasion.

The Wings of Love

(A Tideling)

Cosmic blessings enlighten
heart and soul heighten
the wings of love will pursue.

Romance is complicated
love builds as advocated
the wings of love will pursue.

Relationships grow profoundly
compassion has no boundary
the wings of love will pursue.

The cosmos connects us all
for love to continue forever.

Compassion is love unabated
when wings of love are created.

Victims

(A Sijo)

Life is a struggle for everyone, leaving some in a pall
once a victim, a vicious circle can be created from anger
victims are harmed, they need compassion to recover.

Without compassion love is lost to reverie forever
to grow up on no love leaves souls to demons, nothing else
victims are lost in society, they feel the time to crawl.

Turmoil leaves us all to a time of victimization
coming to grips with life is a struggle for even the best
victims get hurt deep within, hope is needed by all of us.

Lost

(A Tanka)

The mind is a tool
for learning lessons in life
nature teaches us
good from bad in strangest ways
lost is behaving badly.

Clonclurry Parakeet

(A Haiku)

A temperate bird
double clutching Clonclurry
Parakeets need love.

Cosmic Love

(A Sonian)

The cosmos connects us
embracing us all
mystic blessings
cosmic love.

Merging Souls

(A Tideling)

Dating begins relationships
of good romantic partnerships
merging souls creates happiness.

Building relationships honestly

is an alliance consciously
merging souls creates happiness.

Romance needs constancy
love grows biologically
merging souls creates happiness.

Romance is the epitome
of love in cosmic bliss.

Souls need a cosmic connection
making love is the predilection.

Grasping Love

(A Sijo)

Love is a nocturnal place in the subconscious of the mind
everyone tries to understand love, when conscious of time
grasping love can get us hurt, if failing to make love mine.

Love is a place where we look eye to eye to feel sublime
wondering what love is keeps us busy, if losing at romance
grasping love is not easy, it takes learning as we grow up.

Doting leads us on, touching others souls helps us learn
broken hearts can heal, if we learn from mistakes in time
grasping love may cause broken hearts, show compassion.

Back Pain

(A Tanka)

The back gives us strength
physical virility
comes as a blessing
heredity is birthright
back pain kills our love's embrace.

Derbyan Parakeet

(A Haiku)

A bird, shy to touch
great talker and trickster, Der-
byan Parakeet.

Karma

(A Sonian)

What goes round, comes around
when cosmic blessings
chooses payback
love's karma.

Thinking

(A Tideling)

Creativity requires solidarity
making art requires dexterity
thinking requires listening with skill.

Artistry is passionate

love is always compassionate
thinking requires listening with skill.

Development requires dedication
values can create foundation
thinking requires listening with skill.

Listening requires patience and skill
for making sound judgments.

Thinking is a biological skill
we need a listening freewill.

Taming the Soul

(A Sijo)

The soul is wild from the day we are born, so it will grow
learning from nature's ways we should grow into adulthood
taming the soul kills the spirit, baring it keeps love whole.

Romance is birthright, as we mature we want to make love
babies come if life forces are brought to bear on the soul
taming souls may do harm, live life, keeping heart and soul.

Creativity needs an abundance of mental persuasion
building a life is a responsibility for all of us
taming the soul is painful, life needs compassion to grow.

Phony Baloney

(A Tanka)

Guys and gal play games
breaking hearts brings a blame game
Bony Maroney
was sung in the late fifties
phony baloney rips poems.

Border Canary

(A Haiku)

A timid singer
copes with devious antics
Border Canary.

Sour Grapes

(A Sonian)

Hard times brings out anger
the temper turns sour
the soul feels lost
sour grapes.

Stress

(A Tideling)

Anxiety is defiant
patience brings calm reliance
stress is a killer over time.

Pressure becomes tension
loss of proper attention
stress is a killer over time.

Resistance is temperamental
the breaking point elemental
stress is a killer over time.

Hate and anger compete
for attention with raw wounds.

Patience gives keeps us sober
when we find a sound closure.

Politics

(A Sijo)

Rhetoric, the art of persuasion, intelligence overcomes
fighting and bickering are weights on many a good soul
politics is false hope, find truth within your own being.

Religion is a not a good discourse for politicians
it goes against nature's way, souls need to learn lessons
politics can break good people, making them want money.

Money is a problem, watch your pennies, but be generous
know the value of anything you wish to purchase for buying
politics can do harm, know government as if you are blind.

Murky Waters

(A Tanka)

Romance, politics
gets us lost when building trust
we will get confused
losing conscience of the process
murky waters are embraced.

Diamond Dove

(A Haiku)

Easy going bird
tamable and calm
loving Diamond Dove.

Charm and Pomp

(A Sonian)

Romance needs expression
words so passionate
rebel rousing
charm and pomp.

Cousins

(A Tideling)

Relations are ornery
mysticism is sorcery
cousins are loving kin.

Relatives are orderly
the cosmos connects disorderly
cousins are loving kin.

Romance is unpredictable
making love is reciprocal
cousins are loving kin.

First cousins are respectable
seconds are within range.

Love is for all who connect
let go to know what you collect.

Human Bonding

(A Sijo)

Love is unconditional between parent and children
the bond grows apart in time, as children grow, leave home
mankind can be broken, some want no part of home pond.

Love is supposed to develop a long term bond ever more
true love is not practical, that is why we want it all the more
mankind can be easily harmed, use care to make a pond.

Taboos can be tantalizing, avoid what leads to wrong paths
romance is a tool to bring love, bonds can develop strength
mankind is culpable, be careful to grow a strong pond.

Marking Paths

(A Tanka)

Demagogues play games
with other people's lost lives
taking advantage
with no empathy for life
marking paths, pride and glory.

Glouster Canary

(A Haiku)

A bird with a song
pleasant when singing to you
Glouster canary.

Songs of the Wild

(a Sonian)

Indian love calls haunt
both the heart and soul
making love songs
of the wild.

Drifting Through Life

(A Tideling)

Marijuana highs exalting
loss of space resulting
drifting through life as nothing matters.

Getting drunk inebriated

makes one mentally incapacitated
drifting through life as nothing matters.

Natural highs elevate
bringing love to acclimate
drifting through life as nothing matters.

Nature is a gift to us all
not taking care of it is harmful.

A natural high gives us bliss
even lovers will feel amiss.

Privilege and Persuasion

(A Sijo)

Old white men delight in privileges above others
taking advantage of others of a different color
privilege, persuasion leave some cold, pinching pennies.

Wealth breeds false pride, making fear an hate tool to use
wicked ways are in play, evil purposes in mind, ever there
privilege, persuasion do harm, take care in your choices.

Fame and fortune lead to action that treat others like dirt
dress and fashion are obstacles to compassion, fear of loss
privilege, persuasion are tools for harm, use carefully.

Scary Places

(A Tanka)

Halloween brings fear
into minds of young children
but there is terror
in the hearts of adults too
scary places fool the smart.

Goffin's Cockatoo

(A Haiku)

A quiet, peaceful
bird, needing lots of playtime
Goffin's Cockatoo.

Abusing Privilege

(A Sonian)

Privilege is selfishness
when used by mankind
for abusing
privilege.

A Time for Protests

(A Tideling)

Nixon brought impatience
with the presidents complacence
a time for protests and killing resulted.

Vietnam brought horrors
minds wanted peace restorers
a time for protests and killing resulted.

Immigrants held captive
to illegal orders combative
a time for protests and "killing" resulted.

Time and space need relativity
hell is giving a close all.

Protests will come from revulsion
when trust is killed for corruption.

Political Suicide

(A Sijo)

Politics requires soft persuasion, corruption brings protests
Nixon was corrupt, tapes were his downfall, he resigned
political suicide is hurtful, the harm can be widespread.

Vietnam brought protests that led to death of protesters
corrupt plans led to Johnson's failure, he was moving on
political suicide is the wrong path, a path that is revolting.

An executive order rejecting immigrants is not legal at all
anger at other countries, an excuse to rule against Muslims
is political suicide for sure, impeachment is on the horizon.

Loss of Hope

(A Tanka)

Life can be happy
it is a choice we all make
find a happy spot
to live in where love will flow
so loss of hope does not win.

Gold-Breasted Waxbill

(A Haiku)

A healthy tough bird
small and active avian
Gold-Breasted Waxbill.

Rainbows

(A Sonian)

Harsh rhetoric does harm
bringing anger out
rainy days bring
on rainbows.

Practice Teaches Skill

(A Tideling)

Learning has complexity
creativity brings out chemistry
practice teaches us better skill.

Teaching is dependency
students look for destiny
practice teaches us better skill.

Cooperation brings equity
delinquency costs us ecstasy
practice teaches us better skill.

Learning is part of growing mature
teaching is its compliment.

We all need practice to learn skill
along with love and a free will.

Distractions

(A Sijo)

Creativity needs patience and obedience to the task
level headed focus to the project, so success is ahead
distractions are defeatist, ignore what you do not need.

Romance is active in minds, let the heart and soul be kind
compassion is love at its best, show it whenever you can
illusions delude the mind, trust the soul to guide your path.

Relationships are built on trust, be careful in all you do
give and take are beneficial to the course any romance
distractions take us off course, souls know the good ones.

Money

(A Tanka)

Whites all seem wealthy
people see what they want to
believing in myths
taking reason to account
money is a poor excuse.

Gold-Capped Conure

(A Haiku)

A talkative bird
a active and loud player
the Gold-Capped Conure.

Sanctions

(A Sonian)

Acting badly takes guts
requires punishment
sometimes it takes
hard sanctions.

The Joker

(A Tideling)

Jokers are titillated
by laughter activated
the joker may be crying inside.

Laughter draws spectators
crowds can be predators
the joker may be crying inside.

Romance is delectable
the heartbeat is detectable
the joker may be crying inside.

Jokes make a belly jiggle
laughter is contagious.

The joker show its empathy
others may show sympathy.

Demagogues

(A Sijo)

Anger and hate develop the demagogue's personality
to take risks beyond the pale, white nationalism to prevail
demagogues are harmful, be careful around the bad apple.

Hypocrites are sometimes demagogues, but are not always
patience is lost on the demagogue, they have a temper
demagogues can break the mold, watch for pain from afar.

Anger builds up in the demagogue easily, holding grudges
loss of patience too soon, bashing with no common sense
demagogues are dangerous, Hitler showed us evil charm.

Romantic Waves

(A Sonian)

Heartbeats send out feelings
the cosmos connects us
patience can sense
romantic waves.

A Simplified Love

(A Tideling)

Love connects blessings
romance finds heavens
a simplified love.

Hugs and canoodling
brings romance captivating
a simplified love.

Dating and feeding
following and leading
a simplified love.

Laughing and having fun
senses alive in the moonlight.

Dancing in the rain
finding your own grain.

Earth, Wind, Fire.

Waking the Soul

(Loop Poem)

The soul is our guide to love
love connects us cosmically
cosmically love makes us thrive
thrive with love of adventures.

Adventures keep us romantic
romantic times seem to be arcane
arcane moments drive us crazy
crazy life is all we ever have.

Have life as it comes to you
you are blessed by the cosmos
cosmos connects our souls
souls need awakening to grow.

Grow like weeds, earth, fire, wind
wind is a power of love to awaken
awaken the soul when romance thrives
thrives with love, waking the soul.

Bird of South America

(A HAIBUN)

South America is blossoming with romance.
Ancient ways are practiced in many places.
Tribal ways seem arcane to most peoples.
One beautiful bird is the Nanday Conure.

A talented bird
with beauty, good speech mimic
the Nanday Conure.

Winning a Girl's Heart

(A Sonian)

Girls like bold men
following their path
who will get grungy
winning a girl's heart.

Sustaining Heart and Soul

(A Tideling)

Creativity requires heart
artisans do their part
sustaining both heart and soul.

Molding takes talent
artwork is gallant
sustaining both heart and soul.

Painting word pictures
requires mental fractures
sustaining both heart and soul.

The heart is easily broken
compassion fixes the soul.

The soul is the guide for life
with heart we can play the fife.

Earth, wind and Fire!

Tasting Romance

(Loop Poem)

Meeting the tastes of another
another path taken gets nothing
nothing comes from just meeting
meeting is an opportunity for love.

Love brings romance to delight
delight is making love romantic
romantic ways give love its light
light is cosmic bliss without fear.

Fear holds us back from dating
dating keeps the romance lively
lively ways gives a taste of love
love making is what we strive for.

For better or worse is for a life
life gives us zest if we have health
health is critical to tasting romance
romance is an adventure, we resist.

Another Australian Bird

(A HAIBUN)

Australia is wide open spaces with some mountains. Tasmania is part to a continent and other small islands. Deserts are part of its terrain with rivers here and there. One beautiful bird is the Normal grey Cockatiel.

A lovely parrot
lives in Australia, Normal
grey Cockatiel love.

Heart Strings

(A Sonian)

Hearts beat for one
at a time – belongs
to someone special
with heart strings.

Plucking Heart Strings

(A Tideling)

Making the heart yearn
for love making to burn
while plucking heart strings.

Romance is a dance
cupids dart is a lance
while plucking heart strings.

Dating is a feast
angels need a beast
while plucking heart strings.

The heart is easily broken
making up is hard to do.

Romance keeps us going
as long as wild winds are blowing.

Love, life and romance.

Heart and Soul

(Loop Poem)

Hearts can be easily broken
broken relationships do not last
last place is where we may feel
feel the soul to find life's guide.

Guides follow a routine in life
life leads us with nature's ways
ways that teach us lessons over time
time teaches us patience when we learn.

Learn from nature to find your space
space and time lose focus with love
love gives us empathy and compassion
compassion teaches us to sacrifice.

Sacrifice to make others feel good
good comes from love and caring
caring gives us a loving heart and soul
souls need heart to know our place.

Southern Motivated Birds

(A HAIBUN)

Some birds love the southern continent.
Soaring all over Mexico, Central and South America.
Showing their beauty and talents to everyone.
One beautiful bird is the Orange-Chinned Parakeet.

Some birds have talents
mimicking speech and tricks
Orange-Chinned Parakeet.

Cosmic Connections

(A Sonian)

The cosmos connects us
with mystical perfection
love is the promise for
cosmic connections.

Cosmic Romance

(A Tideling)

Romance is cosmic
love making atomic
in true cosmic romance.

Dating seeds deep love
groping is like a shove
in true cosmic romance.

Kissing touches the heart
hugging does its part
in true cosmic romance.

Love is a burning
in the heart and soul.

Romance causes yearning
making love is churning.

Earth, wind, fire!

Cosmic Love

(Loop Poem)

We are all connected cosmically
cosmically we know true love
love is a feeling from the soul
soul is our guide to true romance.

Romance gives us opportunity
opportunity to meet a cosmic soul
soul of one we are meant to meet
meet and merge souls if meant to be.

Be yourself to find your soulmate
soulmate is our cosmic connection
connection to our cosmic love
love that we need to feel complete.

Complete the soul to find true love
love is a cosmic blessing for you
you and me cannot be separated
separated souls are still connected.

Amazonian Birds

(A HAIBUN)

The Amazon runs the length of South America.
Beauty surrounds it in all areas and terrains.
Ancient ways are still practiced along its length.
One beautiful bird is the Orange-Winged Amazon.

Birds flock to rivers
like the Amazon River
Orange-Winged Amazon.

The Nature of Love

(A Sonian)

The Universe teaches us
about love and life
lessons learned about
nature of love.

Nurturing

(A Tideling)

Nature will ensure
life to mature
it is a nurturing process.

The Universe is strange
over galaxies must range
it is a nurturing process.

Worm holes connect parts
black holes break hearts
it is a nurturing process.

Life needs love and nurturing
death is the end of this process.

The cosmos connects us all
the process instills a pall.

Love, life and dearth.

Nurturing Love

(Loop Poem)

Nature tends to nurture romance
romance is healthy for all life
life is a blessing until we pass
pass onto the great beyond in time.

Time is precious teaching us patience
patience is a virtue, learn from nature
nature gives us what we need with health
health is valuable, hang onto love.

Love is blessing to grow into, merge
merge with the cosmos to cherish life
life is our predicament until we die
die we experience in living to the best.

Best we do when we follow our soul
soul is the guide to nurturing love
love gives us hope to a rich future
future is nurturing love in the heart.

Colombian Birds

(A HAIBUN)

Colombia is an ancient land with much beauty.
Incas live there with heritage to ancient times.
The terrain is treacherous and mountainous.
One very beautiful bird is Painted Conure.

A beautiful bird
with many talents and speech
the Painted Conure.

Angelic Souls

(A Sonian)

Souls guide our love
cupid steals hearts
heartbreak hurts
angelic souls.

Broken Hearts

(A Tideling)

Time is healing
love is revealing
broken hearts need compassion.

Romance is enticing
making love is inspiring
broken hearts need compassion.

Meeting with defenses
enables the senses
broken hearts need compassion.

Breaking up may be hard to do
the glue that binds can be like concrete.

Compassion is love and empathy
to keep going we need synergy.

Water, fire, love.

A Sense of the Soul

(Loop Poem)

The soul guides us through life
life thrives when we have passion
passion keeps us going to transcend
transcend the mind to find adventures.

Adventures are healthy for all beings
beings are animal and all of mankind
mankind is destructive, live carefully
carefully go with the winds of change.

Change is the only constant to know
know who you are to balance living
living will awaken all the senses
senses help us learn from nature.

Nature guides us on our path to light
light gives us energy, to keep going
going with light feeds our inner love
love gives us a sense of the soul.

Patagonia in South America

(A HAIBUN)

South America is expansive and ancient in its ways.
The Amazon runs though it with rapids,and muddy waters.
Life is dangerous, the beauty is tremendously lovely
One beautiful bird is the Patagonian Conure.

A talented bird
Patagonian Conures
are beautifully wild.

Challenging the Soul

(A Sonian)

Souls need help to grow
pressures building up
cause stresses to fester
challenging the soul.

Growing the Soul

(A Tideling)

The soul must grow
with the heart in tow
growing the soul takes time.

Hearts can be broken
it is not a token
growing the soul takes time.

Patience is a virtue
growth needs nurture
growing the soul takes time.

The soul is tender
the heart is stressful.

Love begins at birth
life requires mirth.

Fire, water, earth.

Balancing Heart and Soul

(Loop Poem)

The heart needs balance in living
living thrives with balance in love
love needs compassion for growth
growth comes with heart and soul.

Soul is our guide to love and life
life will thrive is we let regrets go
go with love to find your soulmate
soulmate is the lover meant to be.

Be yourself to conquer true love
love thy neighbor, giving and taking
taking only as much to satisfy needs
needs come and go based on balance.

Balance is weighed by heart and soul
soul is a giving nature if love is held
held in the heart, the soul is loving
loving is a balance of heart and soul.

Lovebird of Africa

(A HAIBUN)

Africa is wild and an untamed landscape.
Deserts and mountains cover the terrain.
Beauty is in the eye of the visiting beholder.
One lovely bird is the Peach-Faced Lovebird

Birds love Africa
soaring over the landscape
the Peach-Faced Lovebird.

Nature's Love

(A Sonian)

Nature teaches us life
lessons learned kept
in loving hearts
nature's love.

Nature and Romance

(A Tideling)

Romance in nature
helps us mature
nature and romance go together.

Meeting wildlife teaches
blood is sucked by leaches
nature and romance go together.

Forests protect wildlife
love and life are rife
nature and romance go together.

Nature is universal and cosmic
love connects us mystically.

Romance is an adventure
love has a real censure.

Life, fire and water.

Nature's Way

(Loop Poem)

Nature teaches us how to live
live to the best of your ability
ability is talent to accomplish
accomplish love in your soul.

Soul is the guide to our love
love keeps us going full time
time requires patience to grow
grow with nature's way proving.

Proving the lessons, nature's way
way of the heart is a romance
romance keeps love alive in us
us, a couple, merging hearts, souls.

Souls need love and compassion
compassion keeps us feeling whole
whole is how we feel when together
together we can learn nature's way.

Birds of South America

(A HAIBUN)

South America had many types of wild birds
Some are trainable in speech and doing tricks.
The Amazon is home to many of these wild birds.
One is known as the Peach-Fronted Conure.

A beautiful bird
with fair tricks and smaller words
Peach-Fronted Conure.

Puberty

(A Sonian)

Sexual prowess develops teens
earlier for some than others
yearning for making love
occurs at puberty.

Coming of Age

(A Tideling)

Reaching full puberty
causes tom foolery
sexual prowess is coming of age.

Hugging and kissing
someone you are missing
sexual prowess is coming of age.

Dating is romantic
love grows pedantic
sexual prowess is coming of age.

Making love is on the minds
of the teens and not much else.

Erections and wetness are signs
the cosmos connects our guidelines.

Sex, domination and submission.

Age and Budding Love

(Loop Poem)

Puberty is the coming of age
age is crucial to making love
love is just one of our needs
needs for sex touch our souls.

Souls need compassion with pain
pain is what we have with romance
romance comes when we least expect
expect nothing to find real people.

People will fool you at any age
age of budding love changes
changes in relationships arise
arise with growing sexually.

Sexually active teens need passion
passion comes with puberty in time
time requires patience for virtue
virtue comes with budding love.

Another Australian Bird

(A HAIBUN)

Australia has many terrains and climates.
Deserts and mountains are ancient grounds.
Beauty comes in may forms for all to see.
One lovely bird is the Pearl Mutation Cockatoo.

Birds are plentiful
Australia's Pearl Mutation
Cockatoo love's us.

Stability

(A Sonian)

Life can be stressful
we struggle growing
till we learn nature's way
when we gain stability.

Stable Love

(A Tideling)

Love needs stability
to survive virility
to embrace stable love.

It needs compassion
to embrace deep passion
to embrace stable love.

Romance survives struggles
to overcome our troubles
to embrace stable love.

Embracing love's equality
gives back in many ways.

Give and take embraces romance
if we both do our rain dance.

Rain, fire, love.

Stable Emotions

(Loop Poem)

Emotions cause us trouble
trouble causes us to be angry
angry actions need a release
release is an emotional action.

Action leads to some reaction
reaction comes with a fantasy
fantasy is an emotional mindset
mindset holds us back from duty.

Duty is guided by depths of soul
soul can give us peace of mind
mind hides emotions of peace
peace we need to be stable.

Stable emotions allow true love
love allows emotions compassion
compassion gives us empathy
empathy gives us stable emotions.

Australian Cockatiel

(A HAIBUN)

Australia may be down under, but is unusual.
The East Coast is thriving with large cities.
The west is more ancient and filled with wildlife.
One lovely bird is the Pied Mutation Cockatiel.

Australian bird life
Pied Mutation Cockatiel
soar to find our love.

Sensual Passion

(A Sonian)

Love is sensually aware
with passions awry
loving and caring
sensual passion.

Sensuality

(A Tideling)

Love should be caring
with two souls baring
a full view of sensuality.

Embracing a lover
the cosmos to discover
a full view of sensuality.

Hugging and kissing
someone to be wishing
a full view of sensuality.

Romance is a fancy
leading to be a lover.

Making love is fantasy
bringing to life gravity.

Fire, water, love.

Sensual Romance

(Loop Poem)

Romance should be sensual
sensual love keeps us close
close ties us to the cosmos
cosmos connects us to love.

Love escapes time and space
space is just one of our needs
needs should be met in caring
caring shows others compassion.

Compassion becomes empathy
empathy is true love over time
time is a virtue, give it patience
patience gives us minds in peace.

Peace calms the mind and heart
heart and soul want sensuality
sensuality, love of the best kind
kind words are sensual romance.

India Bird Life

(A HAIBUN)

India is mostly hot and humid, except to the mountains. Love is a prominent feature within each cast grouping. Beauty is found in most areas of the wild landscape. One beautiful bird is the Plum-Headed Parakeet.

India is home
to Plum-Headed Parakeet
a talented bird.

Heartbeats

(A Sonian)

Heart strings need strumming
the heart beats for someone
love makes the heart hum
heartbeats can mean love.

Heartache

(A Tideling)

The heart is fragile
romance will dazzle
heartache is broken romance.

Hearts beat for one
love to be won
heartache is broken romance.

Romance is adventure
the mind should venture
heartache is broken romance.

Hearts can be broken
our love is too fragile.

We live for life and love
heartache to stay above.

Life, love, fire.

Heartache

(Loop Poem)

Hearts are so easily broken
broken hearts take our time
time to heal, and real patience
patience teaches value of love.

Love we all need in growing up
up is better than down to thrive
thrive in love for a good life
life is rich without heartache.

Heartache from a broken heart
heart needs healing to survive
survive with love in the mind
mind is a blessing with peace.

Peace of mind will come in time
time is peaceful when we are kind
kind will keep peace in the heart
heart aches are part of all life.

Another South American Parrot

(A HAIBUN)

Tropical climates are ripe for wild life.
The Amazon is teeming with fish and birds.
Ancient ways are practiced in many places.
One lovely bird is the Quaker Mutation.

South American
birds come in variety
Quaker Mutation.

Fame

(A Sonian)

Seeking fame and fortune
is something all may seek
yet as we grow mature
fame brings grins.

Savoring Romance

(A Tideling)

Romance is enticing
yet struggles are thriving
as we are savoring romance.

Nights out on the town
acting more like a clown
as we are savoring romance.

Hugging and kissing warms
groping comes with transforms
as we are savoring romance.

Romance can be thorny
making love is the goal.

Savoring love is romantic
small gifts and being tantric.

Fire, water, passion.

Familiarity Breeds Contempt

(Loop Poem)

Being overly familiar may breed contempt
contempt comes when love is kept apart
apart we will lose our cosmic connections
connections make us hold onto our love.

Love grows if we keep love in our hearts
hearts make us stronger with a good soul
soul is our guide, nature gives us pathways
pathways to love are part of romantic love.

Love is romantic when life is adventurous
adventurous lives give back in many ways
ways we take, paths to depths of our souls
souls need compassion to maintain the heart.

Heart and soul make music in the cosmos
cosmos connects all if we have open minds
minds are causing the struggles in our lives
lives need real empathy to find true synergy.

Indonesian, Australian Birds

(A HAIBUN)

Indonesia and Australia are warm and tropical.
Warmth and beauty are prolific in many areas.
Climates are seasonal in most places we visit.
One beautiful bird is the Rainbow Lory.

Indonesia and
Australia have many birds
one - Rainbow Lory.

Agony

(A Sonian)

We all get broken hearts
struggling to grow up
when doing our best
agony grabs us.

Connecting with Love

(A Tideling)

Romance is like wrestling
some keep you guessing
connecting with love is a blessing.

Dating testes the heart
how long you stay apart
connecting with love is a blessing.

Hugging and kissing
will you be missing
connecting with love is a blessing.

Romance is cruel
love keeps us guessing.

Cosmic love connects us
we all ride the same bus.

Fire, water, romance.

Enchantment

(Loop Poem)

Romance can be enchanting
enchanting a lover is sweet
sweet is the taste of candy
candy enchants the taste buds.

Buds - friends with who you hang
hang with friends who you value
value love and have good patience
patience is a virtue to romance.

Romance is an adventure in life
life is a reward when you show
show compassion to keep going
going with love in your heart.

Heart and soul are a blessing
blessing is cosmic connection
connection to love is mystical
mystical magic is enchantment.

One more Indonesian Bird

(A HAIBUN)

Indonesia is a tropical haven for wild birds.
Its warmth is giving in ancient, arcane ways.
Beauty is loving and giving in Indonesian ways.
One wild, beautiful bird is the Red Lory.

Indonesian birds
are talented and speak well
the Red Lory loves.

Pain and Passion

(A Sonian)

We all have agony
at times in our lives
love sometimes gives
pain and passion.

Pain of Love

(A Tideling)

Love is painful
peace is a fable
the pain of love stays with us.

Romance is plastic
broken hearts elastic
the pain of love stays with us.

Dating is adventure
love is indenture
the pain of love stays with us.

Love is a cosmic blessing
we all need that connection.

Pain is a sign of passion
love shows some compassion.

Pain, love and fire.

Passion

(Loop Poem)

Passion takes talent and creativity
creativity takes talent and spunk
spunk is what we need to thrive
thrive on love, the heart is tough.

Tough guys will break the heart
heart and soul show how we feel
feel love deep within for romance
romance is painful if we are true.

True love is romantic and giving
giving from the heart is caring
caring with love is passionate
passionate love can be painful.

Painful living can be depressing
depressing the soul can be harmful
harmful ways cause the heart pain
pain is part of love, show passion.

Macaws of South America

(A HAIBUN)

South America has many climates and terrains.
Ancients made practices of Indian musings.
Pyramids were built as testaments to power.
One beautiful bird is the Red-Bellied Macaw.

South America
is filled with wildlife and birds
Red-Bellied Macaw.

Generosity of Soul

(A Sonian)

The heart is forgiving
when love is the goal
romance breeds a
generosity of soul.

Generous Hearts

(A Tideling)

Altruism is uncommon
romance is quite common
a generous heart loves moonlight.

Giving and taking are life
holding back causes strife
a generous heart loves moonlight.

Dating is romantic
small gifts are pedantic
a generous heart loves moonlight.

Romance needs generosity
holding back kills romance.

Generous hearts can find love
the cosmos is higher thereof.

Give, take, passion.

Generous Love

(Loop Poem)

Altruism is uncommon as true love
love needs the cosmos to connect us
us is a couple merging their souls
souls are the guide to our living.

Living is an adventure in romance
romance is dating and holding others
others are part of our lives to thrive
thrive with love touching our hearts.

Hearts are easily broken in affairs
affairs will happen, be forgiving
forgiving is graceful the first time
time needs patience for peacefulness.
Peacefulness comes with generosity
generosity is a path to peace of mind
mind is easily frazzled, be generous
generous love is hard to develop.

Parrots of Africa

(A HAIBUN)

Africa is deserts, mountains and lakes and rivers.
Climate varies according to the wild terrain.
Animal varieties are by particular topography.
One beautiful bird is the Red-Bellied Parrot.

Africa is wild
animal life is varied
Red-Bellied Parrot.

Dying Passion

(A Sonian)

Death comes to all
passion is thriving
love is given to
dying passion.

Embracing Death

(A Tideling)

Embracing love is romantic
small gifts are pedantic
living is embracing death.

Romance is a relationship
it starts with courtship
living is embracing death.

Old age is not scary
life can be hairy
living is embracing death.

Life is a struggle
love is a hard to find.

Romance embraces life
death is a shrew of a a wife.

Death, life, fire.

Life and Death

(Loop Poem)

Life begins a real process
process causes relationships
relationships happen to all
all is a cosmic phenomenon.

Phenomenon brings passion
passion makes babies happen
happen by chance is pure love
love is a dance we do to grow.

Grow with the winds of change
change - the only constant in life
life and death - true complements
complements make love merge.

Merge of two souls is cosmic
cosmic love connects us true
true love is a real connection
connection to love brings death.

South Pacific Birds

(A HAIBUN)

The South Pacific is quite warm and tropical.
The people are warm and cherish romance.
Families are cherished and quite practical.
One beautiful bird is the Red-Sided Eclectus.

South Pacific Birds
love the sun, talented Red-
Sided Eclectus.

Ability to Love

(A Sonian)

Love seems impossible
yet people hold on
for embracing the
ability to love.

Facing Love and Fear

(A Tideling)

Love and fear are perplexing
the heart is always vexing
facing love and fear is painful.

Romance teaches relationships
building romance, a moon eclipse
facing love and fear is painful.

Dating causes fears to arise
the soul is the guide to apprise
facing love and fear is painful.

Fear is an an aphrodisiac
to play is loving and caring.

Love needs fear to create romance
breaking barriers is taking a chance.

Fear, love, fire.

Love, Fear and Fire

(Loop Poem)

Romance is love and fear
fear - an aphrodisiac for love
love is what we seek to give
give and take are equality.

Equality is a journey to thrive
thrive with love and compassion
compassion brings us to be closer
closer we are brings merging souls.

Souls are the guides to pathways
pathways are nature in our lives
lives need nurturing to find love
love gives us empathy and passion.

Passion is fire in depths of our soul
soul guides our heart to find romance
romance leads making love to be true
true love, fear and fire breed romance.

Birds of New Zealand

(A HAIBUN)

New Zealand is mountainous and quite beautiful.
Movies are made there for its climate and terrain.
Passion and creativity are highest in their goals.
One beautiful bird is the Red-Crowned Kakakiri.

New Zealand wildlife
is unique, talented, Red-
Crowned Kakakiri.

Embracing Love

(A Sonian)

Love is a connection
the cosmos is heaven
connecting with it
is embracing love.

Giving Back

(A Tideling)

Life is giving and taking
love comes like bread baking
to show compassion is giving back.

Romance is an adventure
making love we want to censure
to show compassion is giving back.

The heart and soul can thrive
when love comes we feel alive
to show compassion is giving back.

Age is just a number
romance is a dating game.

Wisdom gives us patience
love helps us with relations.

Giving, taking, life.

Openness to Love

(Loop Poem)

An open mind can find love
love is romantic to practice
practice we must to survive
survive to escape the reality.

Reality is a disciple to hell
hell is passion with regrets
regrets can harm the soul
soul guides the lives of all.

All we need is love to thrive
thrive on love and music
music is the soul of giving
giving shows openness to love.

Love gives the heart its passion
passion will thrive if we let it
it is a thing we want in our hearts
hearts need an openness to love.

Australian Cockatoo

(A HAIBUN)

Australia is mostly wilderness for the Aborigines.
Large cities bring civility to most Australians.
Life seems genuine when compassion is shown.
One beautiful bird is the Rose-Breasted Cockatoo.

Down under is parched
wildlife is beautiful, Rose-
Breasted Cockatoo.

Magic

(A Sonian)

Love should be romantic
gifts are good for the soul
hugging and kissing
bring us magic.

The Magic of Love

(A Tideling)

Romance should bring souls together
merging as if by a romantic tether
bringing the magic of love to fruition.

Spending time together becomes sweet
hugging and canoodling as a feat
bringing the magic of love to fruition.

Strolling and holding each others hands
is like music to bestow love with pangs
bringing the magic of love to fruition.

Abuse makes love a failing stance
it kills the romance, as well as love.

Love needs pure magic to succeed
enchantment will cause love agreed.

Magic, Fire, love.

Magic Inspires

(Loop Poem)

Love is a magic inspiration
inspiration gives us true love
love is a guide to bestow
bestow love for real romance.

Romance begins a relationship
relationship matters to families
families need compassion to grow
grow like wildfire, love to give.

Give like winds of change blow
blow your own horn, embracing
embracing love is real magic
magic is inspirational in life.

Life needs the magic of love
love helps us grow to be strong
strong values show our souls
souls need magic that inspires.

Macaws of Central and South Americas

(A HAIBUN)

Central and South America are ancient and wild.
Climate and terrain are quite varied overall.
Wildlife can be dangerous, but loving as well.
One beautiful bird is the Scarlet Macaw.

Birds are talented
Central, South Americas
the Scarlet Macaw.

Actions

(A Sonian)

Decisions can cause reactions
over time they cause
hard headed bashes
and actions.

Actions Vs. Reactions

(A Tideling)

Responses can lead to reactions
division amounts to fractions
actions versus reactions matters.

Wisdom will quite often confound
a penny for thoughts is not profound
actions versus reactions matters.

Think before you act to respond
love is the future of being fond
actions versus reactions matters.

Actions are based on thinking
responding is based on the mind.

Facing responsibility is reacting
being artistic is being exacting.

Action, Reaction, Love!

Actions and Reactions

(Loop Poem)

Responses come from our actions
actions lead to reactions in time
time makes us think about response
response is always a costly reaction.

Reaction comes from an action taken
taken with concern for the responses
responses are crucial to the outcomes
outcomes are a result of reactions.

Reactions will lead to future actions
actions need time to weigh the affects
affects are symptoms of our struggles
struggles give us strength to keep going.

Going forward is not getting behind
behind the power curve can mean losing
losing is winning, when time is crucial
crucial to life is action versus reaction.

Southwestern African Parrots

(A HAIBUN)

Southwest Africa is a haven for hybrid parrots.
The climate is varied and the terrain is mountainous.
Wildlife is varied and temperamentally diverse.
One beautiful bird is the Ruppell's Parrot.

Southwest Africa
is home to talented birds
the Ruppell's Parrot.

Balanced Souls

(A Sonian)

Boys and girls look
in the wrong places
merging souls need
balanced souls.

Balancing Romance and Careers

(A Tideling)

Making love and careers can collide
it takes a stronger love to abide
for balancing romance and careers.

Work and play cause a struggle
schedules we tend to juggle
for balancing romance and careers.

Feasting on each others souls
is like fighting over controls
for balancing romance and careers.

Lace and grace go together
like a tether attached to a pole.

Romance needs balance to work
careers make romance go berserk.

Romance, Fire, Balance.

Romance and Careers

(Loop Poem)

Jobs can interfere with a romance
romance is an adventure in love
love is something we are seeking
seeking love goes against careers.

Careers are not the place for dating
dating is against the rules at work
work and play enhance relationships
relationships need love for success.

Success is a reward for careers
careers need rules to follow
follow the rules to seek rewards
rewards come when you aspire.

Aspire to higher values in romance
romance and careers are sensitive
sensitive souls find soul mates
mates help careers and romance.

South American Conures

(A HAIBUN)

South America is home to the Amazon and wildlife.
The climate varies from very hot to an icy cold.
Wildlife is not tame and the birds are talented.
One beautiful bird is the Sun Conure.

South America
is home to wildlife and birds
the Sun Conure thrives.

Relativity

(A Sonian)

All things are related
pushing, pulling on each other
with masses and gravity
pure relativity.

Relationships with Love

(A Tideling)

Families and friends may collide
we choose who to abide
in our relationships with love.

Romance is an adventure in love
we want romance high as thereof
in our relationships with love.

We spend time with those we cherish
we hope they will never perish
in our relationships with love.

Time teaches us patience
our love is very fragile.

Relationships need a guide
our souls will not be denied.

Love, Romance, Passion.

Tidal Waves

(Loop Poem)

The moon makes waves abide
abide with love to build romance
romance can lead to relationships
relationships are for building family.

Family should lead to unconditional love
love is fragile and may not always last
last in, first out is commonly enough
enough is never quite enough to endure.

Endure to survive the struggles in life
life is nature's path to love's adventure
adventure teaches us how to navigate
navigate the waves to find love's path.

Path is the soul's way to find true love
love is our guide to true romance
romance is made with tidal waves
waves keep us thinking on our feet.

Central American Toucans

(A HAIBUN)

Central America is haven to wildlife and birds.
The climate varies and the terrain is treacherous.
The cultures are warm and dangerous as well.
One beautiful bird is the Swainson's Toucan.

A talented bird
learns tricks, love's to be playful
the Swainson's Toucan.

Hungers

(A Sonian)

We eat as we grow
as we age we seek
a love deep within
hungers to sow.

Taming Hungers

(A Tideling)

Hunger becomes a yearning
growing with souls churning
taming hungers is a plateau.

Eating satisfies our desire
for food we want, a quagmire
taming hungers is a plateau.

Romance creates enticement
we look for love's excitement
taming hungers is a plateau.

Hunger may come and go
regrets go away in time.

Taming hunger is often hard
as hunger is a courtyard.

Hunger, Feet, Fire.

The Hunger Game

(Loop Poem)

Romance makes us hungry
hungry for love making to know
know yourself hold its values
values are the virtue of your life.

Life is a blessing, if you find love
love is what we seek, we have Mothers
Mothers teach us about love of life
life is about learning as we grow.

Grow to reach natural maturity
maturity is wisdom, let it flow
flow like the wild winds of change
change for the better with true love.

Love like a wildfire, burning for life
life is an adventure, do not let it go
go forward to find your desires
desires come with the hunger game.

Indonesian Cockatoos

(A HAIBUN)

Indonesia is warm and people can be hospitable.
The climate is tropical and the terrain varies.
Wildlife is plentiful and some are tamable.
One beautiful bird is the Umbrella Cockatoo.

Indonesian Birds
are tamable, fun, Um-
brella Cockatoo.

Barriers to Love

(A Sonian)

Abuse is not loving
broken hearts are torn
betwixt and between
barriers to love.

Twisted Romance

(A Tideling)

Dating leads to a relationship
love can become like a kinship
twisted romance is sweeter than most.

Hugging and kissing is a start
making love will touch the heart
twisted romance is sweeter than most.

Spending time brings us closer
we become a love broker
twisted romance is sweeter than most.

Love is a path to cosmic bliss
we come together to make love.

Relationships need romance
it portends to keep us in a trance.

Twists, Turns, Fire.

Gnarly Love

(Loop Poem)

Love tends to be twisted
twisted love brings merging
merging souls are soul mates
mates for a sound relationship.

Relationship is what we yearn
yearn for real love to acquire
acquire the best of life and love
love like the winds of wildfires.

Wildfires burn to clear the landscape
landscape is the world we live on
on our time we should give back
back down to show your inner strength

Strength is the mind showing love
love should give us twisted romance
romance teaches us who we need
need drives are inner gnarly love.

Another African Parrot

(A HAIBUN)

Africa is a haven to wildlife, among them birds.
Hunters go there to search for game and meat.
The land is dangerous and varies in climate.
One beautiful bird is the Uncape Parrot.

Africa is wild
talented birds make it home
the Uncape Parrot.

Differences

(A Sonian)

Black, white matters
kaleidoscope skins
sameness is bunk
differences to love.

Common Goals

(A Tideling)

Differences are common as hardships
plants grow wild like tasty parsnips
differences drive us to common goals.

Averages are common as baseballs
making a grand slam enthralls
differences drive us to common goals.

Hate and anger challenge weak minds
love is a challenge for the masterminds
differences drive us to common goals.

We grow up making promises to ourselves
but over time we become overwhelmed.

Goals may give us purpose over time
making do is like a nursery rhyme.

Goals, Fire, Passion.

Differences Matter

(Loop Poem)

Black and white are colors
colors of the rainbow matter
matter is a crucial difference
difference means not the same.

Same is inconsequential to all
all need love and affection
affection is closeness to adore
adore those you love to death.

Death comes too quickly for some
some pass by us not noticing
noticing differences is a sense
sense gives us purpose in love.

Love develops relationships, shields
shields give us comfort in struggles
struggles are part of life's blessing
blessing is a difference that matters.

South Pacific Eclectus

(A HAIBUN)

The South Pacific is tropical and varies in climate.
The terrain can be mountainous and dangerous.
Wildlife is varied and beauty is prominent.
One beautiful bird is the Vosmaeri Eclectus

The South Pacific
is a haven for the Vos-
meari Eclectus.

Fundamental Values

(A Sonian)

Patience is a virtue
in time we mature
growing up with
fundamental values.

The Passion of Love

(A Tideling)

Romance teaches us to hug and kiss
with someone over time we will miss
the value of love is how long it lasts.

Spending time with a partner
encourages our inner armor
the value of love is how long it lasts.

Affection grows as relationships mature
as desires grow, there develops an allure
the value of love is how long it lasts.

Being away causes a longing for bliss
when we miss someone we have yearnings.

Devotion teaches us the value of love
heaven is a higher plain thereof.

Value, Patience, Passion.

A Pack of Wolves

(Loop Poem)

Wolves may howl for soul mates
mates are devoted to one another
another way of sharing is giving
giving love shows our pathway.

Pathway to love is inner depth
depth gives us wisdom and light
light is learning, when we serve
serve each other to show maturity.

Maturity is a place where we believe
believe first in yourself, then help
help those less fortunate with empathy
empathy is compassion for plights.

Plights are part of the struggle in life
life can be a blessing in love's light
light attracts bugs, be their in twilight
twilight brings out a pack of wolves.

Southwestern Australian Birds

(A HAIBUN)

Southwestern Australia is forested and a wealth of beauty. It is a place for catering to the wealthy and has culture. Wildlife is abundant and some are easily tamable. One beautiful bird is the Western Rosella.

Southwest Australia
is a haven for some birds
Western Rosella.

Infatuation

(A Sonian)

Fantasies drive romances
if you fall too fast
in romantic situations
is is infatuation.

Infatuous Love

(A Tideling)

Too soon we can fall
in a love to enthrall
infatuous love is pointless.

Infatuation comes quickly
it ends up being sickly
infatuous love is pointless.

Yearning for a love relationship
is more like a comic strip
infatuous love is pointless.

Comic books are fun to read
romance is not well covered.

When true love touches the soul
we start to begin to feel whole.

Falling, Fast, Decay.

Picking and Choosing

(Loop Poem)

It takes time to find true love
love is very picky about mates
mates need time to acclimate
acclimate slowing for your love.

Love is a blessing over time
time is precious in romance
romance touches mind and soul
soul is our guide to life and love.

Love is what we want to hold
hold a girl in your arms at night
night is romantic when embraced
embraced lovers show their love,

Love is choice like happiness
happiness comes with hugs
hugs need two to be happy
happy picking, choosing love

Deep Love

(A HAIBUN)

The Moment For Love

(A Tanka)

It takes a long time
to find love with a good match
I wait for someone
to appear from the unknown
in the moment now passed by!

A Moment

(A Haiku)

The past did not last
the future will die, unless
a moment comes NOW!

Fluidity

(A Sonian)

Love is a struggle
making it easier
gives romance
its fluidity.

Fluid Romance

(A Tideling)

Romance can be a struggle
with schedules to juggle
compassion shows fluid romance.

Work and play take time
while trying to stay prime
compassion shows fluid romance.

Hugging and kissing are romantic
little gifts shine on the pedantic
compassion shows fluid romance.

Hopping and skipping are fun
feasting on love is not lunch.

Staying fluid gives us motion
romance is full of emotion.

Water, Fire, Love.

Fluid Love

(Loop Poem)

Love is fluidity in emotions
emotions give us our senses
senses tell us how to react
react with real sensitivity.

Sensitivity shows we are real
real love comes from soul depths
depths of the soul can be cruel
cruel love is sometimes romantic.

Romantic adventures are special
special people need our compassion
compassion shows we are kind
kind intentions show our affection.

Affection helps others love grow
grow as you learn about romance
romance is part of accepting love
love is fluid when we do our part.

Birds and Bees

(A HAIBUN)

Birds

(A Tanka)

Birds have a sweet song
chirping like a woodpecker
pecking to find food
making holes as proceed
love gives them higher esteem.

Bee Hives

(A Haiku)

Bees love wild flowers
taking pollen for honey
a bee hive of love.

Focusing Love

(A Sonian)

Romance is a scramble
it takes time to find peace
patience is a virtue
for focusing love.

Romance in Focus

(A Tideling)

Dating is like scrambled eggs
love is romance with legs
romance in focus is strong love.

Hugging and kissing is a seed
making love is a sexual need
romance in focus is strong love.

Building a relationship shows love
bridging the gaps in it thereof
romance in focus is strong love.

Broken hearts happen easily
the give and take of romance.

To focus on romance brings hope
to focus gives romance its scope.

Focus, Passion, Love.

Focus on Love

(Loop Poem)

Losing focus on relationships
relationships are built on love
love is a blessing with might
might gives us inner strength.

Strength is important to light
light is the cosmos connecting
connecting our love together
together we emerge as couples.

Couples make romance heaven
heaven is here on earth as light
light gives us love when we give
give and take show more equality.

Equality is a focus on romance
romance keeps our focus on love
love gives us balance to fight
fight for focus on true love.

Breathing

(A HAIBUN)

A Natural High

(A Tanka)

Nature gives us life
we learn from laws of nature
to inhale, exhale
breathing so we stay alive
creativity – talent.

Air

(A Haiku)

We all need to breathe
we inhale, exhale, aware
fresh air, flowers bloom.

Myth

(A Sonian)

Ancients gave us magic
told tales to enchant
mystifying the mind
with Pagan Myth.

Myth and Magic

(A Tideling)

Myth comes from ancients
they had little patience
myth and magic paves the way.

Magic comes from imagination
creative ways need foundation
myth and magic paves the way.

Tragedy and comedy compete
plays are paid for by the elite
myth and magic paves the way.

Myth and magic create plays
for entertainment to be enjoyed.

Magic is love and romance
myths make a good trance.

Myth, Magic, Fire.

Mythical Forces

(Loop Poem)

Myths came from ancients to play
play with fire and you may get pain
pain is what we feel, lacking foresight
foresight gives us a clue to the future.

Future events occur no matter our intent
intent portends of what is meant to be
be yourself to give your soul freedom
freedom is a state of peace in the mind.

Mind depends on heart, the soul guides
guides us to be ourselves on our paths
paths lead our way to finding love
love is our blessing when we give.

Give and take in life can give equality
equality makes a relationship is sound
sound couples make romance relate
relate to mythical forces for true love.

Myth and Magic

(A HAIBUN)

Magic

(A Tanka)

Love can be tragic
yet love is magic's path
through both thick and thin
tragedy leaves us breathless
magic will embrace the soul.

Myth

(A HAIKU)

Myth comes from ancients
pagan rituals bring love
magic is its lane.

Lost Energy

(A Sonian)

Love gives us passion
struggles wear us down
defeatism causes
loss of energy.

Age and Passion

(A Tideling)

Age is just a number
romance is a wonder
age and passion can grow.

Time may give us wisdom
patience gives us rhythm
age and passion can grow.

Romance is an adventure
aging gives us a texture
age and passion can grow.

Aging helps us as does nature
learning helps us with growth.

Passion grows with learning
love grows with our observing.

Age, Passion, Light.

Aging and Wisdom

(Loop Poem)

Aging should be full of adventures
adventures can be cut short of time
time teaches us patience for romance
romance teaches us about love and sex.

Sex and passion go together like glue
glue of the heart and soul take spine
spine is the backbone of romance
romance keeps life in relationships.

Relationships need nurturing to gel
gel is the better part of affection
affection holds couples together
together we do better than apart.

Apart we miss each other more
more affection holds partnerships
partnerships need growth and love
love takes mature age and wisdom.

Love is Magic

(A HAIBUN)

Magic of Love

(A Tanka)

Love is cosmic bliss
romance - a journey of love
can be a struggle
affection will win the heart
the soul is the guiding force.

Mastering Love

(A HAIKU)

Magic is master
of embracing essence of
love, birds and bees know.

Friends

(A Sonian)

Affection develops slowly
struggles get in the way
when devotion comes
we are friends.

Enemies

(A Tideling)

Friends can become cheaters
real friends are keepers
enemies hide their feelings.

Politics is a breeder
of anger, a hate feeder
enemies hide their feelings.

Religions develop fears
it estranges our peers
enemies hide their feelings.

Hate feeds twisted ideals
enemies will ruin the day.

Enemies need compassion
they want to harm passion.

Fear, Hate, Fire!

Friends Versus Enemies

(Loop Poem)

Enemies hide their feelings
feelings of love make friends
friends stand firmly for you
you need love, not enemies.

Enemies you need closer
closer than friends to trust
trust will show genuine love
love will push away enemies.

Enemies will try to harm souls
souls are the guide to our lives
lives need passion to connect
connect with cosmic energy.

Energy comes from the soul
soul with heart brings friends
friends show you affection
affection disarms enemies.

Affection

(A HAIBUN)

Love needs compassion
to bring two people closer
hugs make us feel warm
over time we may fall in
love and affection is blessed.

Bears

(A Haiku)

Burly animals
with warm fur for keeping warm
teddy bears love hugs.

Forsaken Love

(A Sonian)

Romance is a struggle
love ebbs and flows
patience giving out
is forsaken love.

Making a Commitment

(A Tideling)

Love needs time and good treatment
missing a lover can be malignant
making a commitment takes a long time.

Romance can be good for the soul
making love may make you feel whole
making a commitment takes a long time.

Passion can lead to good creativity
life and nature need a touch of reality
making a commitment takes a long time.

Marriages do not always work out
broken hearts are a slice of pie.

Sticking by one another is persistent
when true love comes, commitment.

Fire, Water, Desire!

Devotion

(Loop Poem)

Marriage takes real commitment
commitment is passion to abide
abide your soul, to find true love
love protects the heart and soul.

Soul is the guide to deep affection
affection touches the heartstrings
heartstrings need strumming to beat
beat like a humming bird in love.

Love - a blessing, hold it to the light
light is love when we find its blessings
blessings touch the soul with devotion
devotion builds trust and romance.

Romance touches depths of souls
souls connects with cosmic light
light allows true inner emotions
emotions bring out innate devotion.

Origami

(A HAIBUN)

Paper folded love
shaped to show a rose budding
made by girls and boys
romantic folded paper
shows devotion in romance.

Paper Dolls

(A HAIKU)

Folding of a bird
made with paper affection
hummingbirds show love.

Cosmic Bliss

(A Sonian)

Romance is a heaven
bringing passion down
to a level of
cosmic bliss.

Heavenly Bliss

(A Tideling)

Romance is passion for two
two makes a couple cuckoo
making love is heavenly bliss.

Spending time together makes blue
when we miss each other we are glue
making love is heavenly bliss.

Distance is a love factor
do not be a lonely detractor
making love is heavenly bliss.

Keep love in the heart always
keep romance on fire forever.

Grow love in your heart and soul
it will always make you feel whole.

Love, Passion, Bliss!

Heaven in Heart and Soul

(Loop Poem)

The soul guides us to love and life
life can be a blessing or a struggle
struggle as we may nature has time
time requires patience to find love.

Love connects us with the cosmos
cosmos connects the moon and stars
stars are a guide to heavenly bliss
bliss we feel when we know light.

Light is love, though minds juggle
betwixt and between the twilight
twilight is for vampires to breed
breed for love, when it seems right.

Right is a truth we seek for why
why is a never ending question
question what matters to love
love is heaven in heart and soul.

Butterflies

(A HAIBUN)

Butterflies are Free

(A Tanka)

Life is a struggle
we all want love, to belong
greed gets in the way
we can have it all in time
stomach butterflies are free.

Butterflies

(A Haiku)

Worms become beauty
flying off in the sunshine
butterflies are free.

Conscious Allure

(A Sonian)

The mind wants magic
to make love shine
enchanted love is
conscious allure.

Enchanted Moments

(A Tideling)

Some moments are magical
to enchant a soul is radical
enchanted moments are heaven's door.

Patience needs virtue and love
compassion is giving thereof
enchanted moments are heaven's door.

Time and space can go away
enchantment has its own sway
enchanted moments are heaven's door.

Reality is a path to actual events
love needs a charmed embrace.

Romance brings magic components
in time come enchanted moments.

Time, Passion, Fire!

Moments in Reverie

(Loop Poem)

Time and space are enchanted
enchanted moments appear
appear out of a crystal ball
ball holds a spell on souls.

Souls are the guides to life
life is a capsule to behold
behold illusions to find love
love gives us energy to live.

Live for love of good times
times can be enchanted love
love connects the cosmos to us
us is two with love's reverie.

Reverie is love's enchantment
enchantment holds the chains
chains hold the heart to love
love gives moments in reverie.

Cats

(A HAIBUN)

Black Cats

(A Tanka)

Black cats are scary
the world is more sinister
angels show us love
tigers are striped with danger
eat pancakes to find their love.

Panthers

(A Haiku)

Black cats are Panthers
the seek love in the twilight
Panthers eyes shine love.

Gender Senses

(A Sonian)

The smell, taste and passion
are different for the sexes
submit, dominate play
offer gender senses.

Gender Sensations

(A Tideling)

The sexes are different in persuasions
the senses offer us chemistry equations
gender sensations come from moonlight.

The tides turn for menstrual bleeding
men pursue women for their seeding
gender sensations come from moonlight.

Romance is an embracing love adventure
making love is a passionate pleasure
gender sensations come from moonlight.

The sexes connect with the cosmos
love bonds us with the moonlight.

Genders differ for good reason
when breeding love is in season.

Sex, Passion, Fire.

Sense of a Woman

(Loop Poem)

A woman needs a man's seed to breed
breed for a woman is the ultimate act
act like a man to find love with women
women like men to show them real love.

Love attracts a woman to men like a trap
trap a woman with enchantment to keep
keep a woman loving you with man's heat
heat holds warmth like real affection.

Affection will show a woman you love her
her faith in men is based on being his light
light of love comes from the moon above
above is heaven when there is moonlight.

Moonlight shines to control menstrual flow
flow with the wild winds in the twilight
twilight brings vampires to bloods flow
flow needs seed to find her lover's goal.

Bounds of Romance

(A HAIBUN)

Romance

(A Tanka)

Love is a struggle
we tangle, hold on
till we make love right
we dominate and submit
till making love ends the race.

Love is....

(A Haiku)

Dancing in the rain
basking in the sunshine, and
loving of wild winds.

Dreaming

(A Sonian)

Sleep awakens the subconscious
in REM sleep we walk
amongst the clouds
we are dreaming.

Dreams of Romance

(A Tideling)

Sleep brings dreams of love making
the subconscious brings on shaking
dreams of romance make us quake.

Daydreams come all of a sudden
like the pushing of a button
dreams of romance make us quake.

Dreams at night are prophetic
making love seems poetic
dreams of romance make us quake.

Dreams help us find answers
a sudden enlightenment.

Our dreams help our vision
in helping make a decision.

Dreams, Vision, Life.

Dream Visions

(Loop Poem)

Vision comes to us in our dreams
dreams help us to make decisions
decisions are important to our lives
lives matter till the end of time.

Time makes us impatient for love
love keeps us connected cosmically
cosmically we find true romance
romance teaches how to make love.

Love fills our dreams with flirting
flirting feeds our hormonal pathways
pathways to love come from dreams
dreams seed our subconscious soul.

Soul is the guide to love and life
life comes from nature and dreams
dreams are the seeds of good fortune
fortune is based on dream visions.

Songs of Love

(A HAIBUN)

Our Song

(A TANKA)

In our depths a song
tells the soul's story of love
nature teaches us
a path to find love in life
we will find love with our song.

Songs

(A HAIKU)

Birds chirp a love song
to find a mate, given time
birds and bees know love.

Long Term Friendship

(A Sonian)

Friends can come late
making the best friends
peace and love test
long term friendship.

Best Friends

(A Tideling)

Friends come and go over time
school chums are liked in the prime
best friends want each other, to embrace.

Peace and love show friendship true
when away friends will miss you
best friends want each other, to embrace.

Friendship should be like nature's path
holding each other dear without wrath
best friends want each other, to embrace.

A friend holds you next to the heart
wanting the best in life forever.

Strong friendship is true to the soul
best friend will make you feel whole.

Friends, Peace, Love!

Friends and Acquaintances

(Loop Poem)

Good friendships develop with flow
flow with the wild winds of change
change when you need to over time
time requires patience from the soul.

Soul is the guide to peace and love
love we need to maintain values
values keep us strong and moral
moral paths are nature's pathway.

Pathway to the heart is true love
love and peace connect the cosmos
cosmos is what connects our souls
souls need friends to embrace.

Embrace your soul mate as a friend
friend is betwixt and between us
us is a friendship growing wise
wise is a friend, acquaintances go.

Trees

(A HAIBUN)

Families

(A Tanka)

Families make a tree
we help each other find love
free as birds and bees
ancient trees connect with peace
giving, taking cosmically.

Ancient Trees

(A Haiku)

Trees are meant to grow
old without being cut down
ancient trees enthrall.

Cages

(A Sonian)

Chains we hold onto
like building blocks
we play with as kids
become our cages

Cages of the Mind

(A Tideling)

The mind is a mystery
we learn about history
building cages of the mind in time.

Wisdom comes from nature
lessons we learn as we mature
building cages of the mind in time.

Enlightenment is sudden
with sleep as a push button
building cages of the mind in time.

Our jobs are part of our cage
we work at breaking it apart.

Life is nature's pathway
we build cages part of the way.

Minds, Cages, Love!

Enchanted Cages

(Loop Poem)

Love helps us build cages
cages hold us to commitment
commitment drives us insane
insane is relief from our duty.

Duty is good for the soul
soul is our guide in living
living is a blessing with love
love makes us feel more whole.

Whole is four quarters, divide
divide life and love in its parts
parts become a magic cages
cages keep us safe from harm.

Harm comes into every life
overcoming harm are struggles
struggles make us learn of love
love needs enchanted cages.

Roads

(A HAIBUN)

Souls need a pathway
a road to follow in life
finding love to hold
making life better, sublime
the road less taken survives.

Roads Less Taken

(A HAIKU)

Highways and byways
nature's lessons teach us life
the roads less taken.

Egos

(A Sonian)

Feeling high on oneself
holding yourself better
than others can be
egos will deceive.

Ego and Self-esteem

(A Tideling)

We all need to feel good
do not wait for Robin Hood
the ego needs self-esteem and love.

Romance should stroke egos
hugs and kisses in love's throes
the ego needs self-esteem and love.

Success is based on how you feel
real love is based on sex appeal
the ego needs self-esteem and love.

The ego needs to be stroked
when low needs a pick me up.

Self-esteem grows with the ego
letting go of regrets, love to bestow.

Highs, Lows, Depth!

Playing the Ego

(Loop Poem)

Egos can be stroked to feel good
good is how we want to grow up
up with the eyes for high esteem
esteem we show to others with love.

Love is a pleasure when we give
give from the heart, not role play
play with egos if you want to fight
fight for what you own, save face.

Face up to responsibilities on time
time and patience grow the ego
ego is good when we give love
love connects us all cosmically.

Cosmically we connect with love
love is a blessing when we embrace
embrace with love in your heart
heart and soul keep egos true.

Atomic Structures

(A HAIBUN)

Molecules are live
structures in making compounds
atomic products
can evolve into new paths
to chemical composites.

Atoms

(A Haiku)

A nucleus formed
surrounded by electrons
atoms charge with chi.

Fun

(A Sonian)

Life is a struggle
fears in our way
till we overcome
and have fun.

Funny Faces

(A Tideling)

Movies bring is novel ideas
life comes at us in bits and pieces
we all make funny faces with love.

Masks we wear give some clues
to who we are though hide the blues
we all make funny faces with love.

Fake smiles are easy to detect
the darker side does reflect
we all make funny faces with love.

Though we try to be funny
we may act like a dunce.

Funny faces can be genuine
sour pusses are like a brine.

Masks, Smiles, Love.

Feeling Enchanted

(Loop Poem)

Life is a struggle when we feel down
down is a place like going downtown
downtown has neon lights, dancing
dancing in the rain is enchantment.

Enchantment comes when we believe
believe in yourself to know your soul
soul is the guide to our true life
life is enchanted when we give love.

Love is magic, enchanted lives begin
begin to love now, let go of regrets
regrets hold us back, give us frowns
frowns give us look like failures.

Failures teach us lessons to learn
learn from past mistakes, to own
own your heart and soul, enchant
both to show love is embraced.

Teardrops

(A HAIBUN)

A Lonely Teardrop

(A Tanka)

I sit and atone
for a love that once went wrong
time eases the pain
losing passion in love's glow
a lonely teardrop now reigns!

Teardrops

(A HAIKU)

Teardrops like raindrops
make the mind pound, as insane
rooftops are its drain.

Reflections

(A Sonian)

Hearts need reverie
a time to think
of sweeter times
good reflections.

Reflections on Life

(A Tideling)

As we age, memories we hold dear
are reverie without any peer
reflections on life to behold.

Romance is something we love
what we think is high above
reflections on life to behold.

Cloudy days bring back memories
the twilight seeks our remedies
reflections on life to behold.

Regrets are a source of pain
reflect on what we should do.

Reverie is a place for reflections
there is no time for corrections.

Reflect, Love, Fire!

Age and Reflections

(Loop Poem)

With age comes our reverie
reverie brings back good times
times we hold dear, missing
missing how we felt back then.

Then and now come together
together is a place in the heart
heart is where we have reflections
reflections move us to feel love.

Love keeps us going in life
life is a blessing in memory
memory helps our reflections
reflections keep us going.

Going forward is our passion
passion touches heart and soul
soul is our guide to living
living gives us age in reflections.

Healthy Souls

(A HAIBUN)

Healing

(A Tanka)

Restoring one's faith
letting go of pain and doubt
nurturing the soul
expelling forces that harm
accepting what's meant to be!

Souls

(A HAIKU)

Life guides are needed
for life to be blessed with grace
nurturing all souls.

Aging

(A Sonian)

We age as we grow
we sense age early on
age catches up with us
as aging senses death.

Our Sense of Age

(A Tideling)

When young we want be older
the Winters may seem colder
our sense of age getting old.

Middle age is time for working
playing around is its shirking
our sense of age getting old.

Our elderly years are coming
in time we begin humming
our sense of age getting old.

The mind can stay young
as the body gets older.

A young mind is bold
though the body will scold.

Youth, Age, Fire.

Aging with Grace

(Loop Poem)

Aging should teach us to be wise
wise is the owl keeping in sight
the values nature teaches in lore
lore keeps our minds in the light.

Light is love when we embrace
embrace what nature teaches us
us is a cosmic connection light
light we need to keep learning.

Learning comes from nature
nature teaches us wise lessons
lessons we need to grow old
old is a number, find wisdom.

Wisdom comes from nature
nature teaches us our paths
paths teach us grace in life
life is about aging with grace.

Fresh Air

(A HAIBUN

Fresh Air

(A Tanka)

Love is a blessing
inspires us to do better
inhale and exhale
replenishing our pathways
fresh air is love's potential.

Fresh Air

(A Haiku)

Rain freshens the air
the taste of love born within
refreshing the soul.

Duty

(A Sonian)

Men and women play roles
showing love as they play
nurturing each others goals
it is a lovers duty.

Duty with Love

(A Tideling)

Romance shares love as the goal
in time dating takes its toll
our duty with love makes romance worthwhile.

Dating is spending time together
it becomes like a lover's tether
our duty with love makes romance worthwhile.

Showing love with hugs and kisses
there are times that seem suspicious
our duty with love makes romance worthwhile.

Duty comes with responsibilities
staying in touch is but one duty.

Love is romantic when we show love
seeing each other in a heaven above.

Duty, Love, Passion!

Duty and Devotion

(Loop Poem)

Being devoted is a lover's duty
duty is responsibility to love
love carries us through hard times
times get hard in struggles we face.

Face of love is devotion to fate
fate is cosmic bliss in an embrace
embrace each other for true love
love like winds of change grow.

Grow love with words of bliss
bliss comes when making love
love grows with our devotion
devotion will keep love alive.

Alive is the heart and soul as one
one is two when there is devotion
devotion is a romance for two duty
duty connects devotion to the cosmos.

Home

(A HAIBUN)

Home

(A TANKA)

In our heart is love
for where nature taught lessons
love we cannot lose
giving and taking, sharing
where the heart goes is our home.

Home

(A HAIKU)

The heart is our path
animals - cosmic partners
find homes in nature.

My Song

(A Sonian)

With my heart filled with love
my soul cannot go wrong
my soul has its
own song.

Singing My Song

(A Tideling)

I am humming to get through
life and loves with skies of blue
singing my song to stay on my path.

A song fills my heart and soul
it keeps me from feeling woe
singing my song to stay on my path.

Love is a song in my heart
it shows me paths to impart
singing my song to stay on my path.

Music steals my heart each day
I lean into the winds of change.

I follow my own song, work and play
it helps me with love to convey.

Sing, Passion, Fire!

Music and Soul

(Loop Poem)

With love in the mind and heart
heart and soul will make time
time for embracing new music
music changes the daily mood.

Mood is an emotion in play
play your own song in life
life tries to meet our needs
needs change as we live.

Live with a song in the heart
heart gives us pleasure of soul
soul is our guide in living
living with love is music.

Music of the soul is discipline
discipline is a choice we make
make the best of love and life
live is music if we show soul.

Music and Love

(A HAIBUN)

Music and Love

(A TANKA)

Love creates romance
dancing in the rain is sweet
romance is dreamland
each person has its own song
music and love to embrace.

Music

(A HAIKU)

Romance is music
beast and beauty have a song
bees buzz and birds chirp.

Fear

(A Sonian)

Death is scorn of life
it comes without warning
we succumb to love
fear is futile.

Lost Loves

(A Tideling)

Lost love is a broken heart
missing someone when apart
lost loves are due to growing fear.

Romance is a struggle in life
marrying someone is a wife
lost loves are due to growing fear.

Sensuality is a lovers best goal
making love makes us feel soul
lost loves are due to growing fear.

Staying in touch is embracing love
when we kiss and hug to show it.

Losing love is due to fear
embracing love is to adhere.

Love, Passion, Fire!

Facing Fears

(Loop Poem)

Fear loses love's commitment
commitment is embracing love
love is what we need to survive
survive in spite of others do.

Do good for better, not for fear
fear keeps us off guard in life
life is nature's way to teach us
us is a couple as free spirits.

Spirits are free when we give
give from the heart, love life
life is good when we give love
love is little good when we fear.

Fears do damage on its own
own up to responsibility to show
that you have love in your heart
heart and soul make fear disappear.

Fear Factors

(A HAIBUN)

Fear Factors

(A Tanka)

Bright lights attract minds
greed, vanity, fears and lies
will darken the soul
fear factors weigh on the heart
overcome from love within!

Fear

(A HAIKU)

Commitment can die
nature teaches us to grow
fears make us defy.

Fate

(A Sonian)

Time can be a killer
we wait for our time
destiny leads
our due fate.

Fatal Obsessions

(A Tideling)

Obsessions can can be manic depression
love can harbor an awkward expression
fatal obsessions can lead to false love embracing.

Hate and love are opposing forces
obsessions come from different sources
fatal obsessions can lead to false love embracing.

Romance is not obsessive like a wild wind
the heart is always ready to find a bend
fatal obsessions can lead to false love embracing.

Waiting indicates an ability of patience
compassion is the embracing of love.

Giving and taking show equal treatment
giving love allows for appeasement.

Fate, Passion, Love!

Respect

(Loop Poem)

Compassion shows signs of deference
deference allows others to oppose
oppose what is bad for your soul
soul is our guide to good living.

Living with love in your heart is kind
kind is giving love that we embrace
embrace love in the heart to profess
profess your own goals to show love.

Love like the winds of change blow
blow your own horn over time
time leads us to show real respect
respect is love of life for others.

Others have the same chances
chances come and go as the wind
wind is blowing as we motivate
motivate others to show respect.

Fate

(A HAIBUN

Facing Life

(A TANKA)

Life is a struggle
standing on your own two feet
is hard for some folks
money makes it easier
facing life gives self-esteem.

Fate

(A HAIKU)

Obsessions grow cold
birds and bees sense innately
a fate is deadly.

87978592R00129

Made in the USA
San Bernardino, CA
09 September 2018